Depression Through A Biblical Lens

Depression Through A Biblical Lens:

A Whole-Person Approach

Ambassador International
GREENVILLE, SOUTH CAROLINA & BELFAST, NORTHERN IRELAND

www.ambassador-international.com

Depression Through A Biblical Lens
A Whole-Person Approach

ISBN: 978-1-62020-265-4
eISBN: 978-1-62020-366-8

Cover Design by Josh Frederick
Ebook Conversion by Anna Raats

AMBASSADOR INTERNATIONAL
Emerald House
427 Wade Hampton Blvd.
Greenville, SC 29609, USA
www.ambassador-international.com

AMBASSADOR BOOKS
The Mount
2 Woodstock Link
Belfast, BT6 8DD, Northern Ireland, UK
www.ambassadormedia.co.uk

The colophon is a trademark of Ambassador

Contents

Introduction

Come with me as we enter into Jane's world. Jane[1] and her husband sought help in regard to bad feelings she was experiencing and the intense desire to have them gone. As I listened intently, Jane told me that most of her life had been characterized by a strong desire to fit in, to feel wanted and be loved, especially by her father. Her mother's approval was just not satisfying. She wanted more. The more she wanted and sought approval, the more elusive it became. Jane grew increasingly embittered and resentful. Actually, she embittered herself. Eventually, she did her own thing and distanced herself from her family. As a result, Jane grew more lonely and upset.

Jane was a believer, but she had become involved in God-displeasing, sinful activities, which only caused more bad feelings. Marriage and children followed, and her bad feelings intensified. Fear, worry, and depression

---

1   Names and case details have been changed.

became a patterned way of life. She feared she would hurt somebody, especially her children. She wanted off the rollercoaster of bad feelings, but did not know how to stop. Jane was a nurse, so she assumed that the Medical Model explained her bad feelings.[2] Several physicians diagnosed her as having a panic disorder, an anxiety disorder, and depression. She was given medications, but the bad feelings kept increasing. Heavily burdened and as a last resort, she came to see me. What would I say and what would I do?

As I heard Jane's story, I asked her to tell me about her most prevalent thoughts and desires, both from earlier years and presently. Jane was eager and intelligent, but she failed to realize that her bad feelings and the desire for relief were ruling her. As a result, she did not want to address her thoughts and desires. Her only goal was freedom from the bondage of bad feelings. She wanted me to help her use the Bible to accomplish that goal.

The initial session set the stage for helping Jane to assess her whole person in terms of her *thoughts, desires,* and *actions*. As we unpacked her story through a biblical grid,

---

2   Three models of disease are discussed in my books *Being Christian in Your Medical Practice* and *True Competence in Medicine* and in my teaching notes on my website, jimhalla.com. With regard to the Medical Model, Koch and Pasteur related the cause of disease to a specific etiologic agent. According to the Medical Model, symptoms and signs are due to a problem with the body (see discussion later in the book regarding Symptoms and Signs). The approach is to treat a presumed body problem, even if one is not found. Also see footnote 20.

hope took on a different perspective. She learned that she was a very controlling person. Jane did not like the parents God had given her, and she had let God know that. She wanted things her way and did not like God's "no." She lived by the rule of "I want" and "I deserve," which led to more bad feelings. In addition, as a part of her effort to control, she was legalistic and performance-oriented. Consumed with self-effort, she read her Bible, prayed, and did good works. But the bad feelings intensified to the point where she felt overwhelmed.

Jane and I met often, and initially the sessions were intense. Jane was burdened, but slowly grasped the concept that she was a whole person redeemed by the blood of the Lamb. As such, her thoughts, desires, and actions were also involved and needed to be addressed. She came to realize that thoughts, desires, actions, and feelings were integrally linked. As we discussed her "bad feelings," their origin, and her response to them, she told me that her anger and resentment had been directed both toward God and toward others. She agreed that she had been depressing herself. The realization of these facts was a major step in helping her get victory.

During our sessions, I often had to tell Jane, "Whoa!" (This is a great discipling word when properly applied.) By God's grace, she learned to "whoa" herself, God's way, for His glory in order to please Him, simply because He was God. She learned the value of a spiritual inventory. She acknowledged for the first time who God truly is and how she had responded sinfully to Him both before and after salvation. She acknowledged the disconnect between her professed faith and her practiced faith. She understood the connection between thinking, wanting, doing, and feelings. That fact alone was a major blessing, and was vital to her gaining victory. Jane was humbled. She had learned to use her dreaded unpleasantness (bad feelings and her situations) to please God by becoming more like Christ. Increasingly, she used her bad feelings to accomplish the greatest activity this side of heaven: becoming more like Christ.

I asked Jane to read this manuscript and comment on it. Her comments were a further encouragement to publish this book. This book gives, I believe, a biblical rationale for approaching people who have been given psychological labels. It is in part an apologetic, calling for a biblically-based practice of medicine and of counseling.

Personal Reflection

Change is an integral part of life, and all people are becomers: that is, we are always in the process of becoming something. Every person is changing and growing more into either the likeness of Christ or the likeness of Satan. Biblically-speaking, non-believers are in the kingdom and family of Satan, and while members of his kingdom, they grow more and more in his likeness (Matt. 13:38; John 8:44; Acts 13:10; 1 John 3:8–12; Eph. 2:1–3). In contrast, at regeneration, believers are radically and supernaturally changed. They are transferred from the kingdom and family of Satan and placed into the kingdom and family of God (Col. 1:13–14; John 3:3–8). Regeneration ushers in a radical change in the heart. As a result of the work of the indwelling Holy Spirit, Christians continually change, becoming more like Christ (Rom. 8:28–29; 2 Cor. 5:9; 2 Pet. 3:18).

The reason man was created is not found in man. Man, an image bearer of God, was created to worship and glorify God (1 Cor. 10:31; Rev. 4:11). However, Adam sinned, and all people were judged in Adam. As a result of God's judgment, man was placed in a deadly and precarious position. The answer to question 18 of the Westminster Shorter Catechism states man's condition and position well: "the sinfulness of the first estate where into man fell consists in the *guilt* of Adam's *first* sin, the *want* [lack] of original righteousness and the *corruption* of his whole nature, together with all actual *transgressions* which proceed from it" (italics mine).

Unsaved man has no desire, will, or ability to please God (Rom. 8:5–8; Eph. 2:1–3). Rather, self takes center stage, expressed as "I want" and "I deserve," which come from the mindset of "what's in it for me?" Unsaved man competes with God in God's world by attempting to establish his own rules. He trusts in himself at his own expense. He lives out of Satan's initial and irrational counsel: "sinning is the best and only way to get ahead. Trust me" (my paraphrase of Genesis 3:4–5; the same thought is expressed in Proverbs 8:36; 12:15; 14:12; and 16:2, 25).

The Fall did not change God's creational design or purpose for man. Instead, the bad news, partially described in the paragraphs above, provided the backdrop for the awesome display of God's good news: His goodness, mercy, and love *and* His holiness, righteousness, and justice. God's love and justice are magnificently and preeminently displayed at the cross. Jesus's perfect

obedience led to His perfect death as the substitution-
ary sacrifice for His people. His work on the cross was
affirmed by His resurrection (Rom. 3:21–26; 4:25; 1
Cor. 1:18–21; 15:1–3). As a result of salvation, hostility
between God and man ceased, relationships were recon-
ciled, and former enemies became children of the King.

In my practice of medicine and ministry of counseling,
I regularly encounter people demonstrating effects of the
Fall. Often they have been given various psychological
labels. Throughout the book I use the terms "psychological labels" and "psychiatric labels" interchangeably
because the terms are ingrained in culture. I believe
the term "feelings states" is a biblically-derived one and
should replace them. I have pondered how to *minister*
to them. One of my goals in this book is to help all
Christians, especially Christian physicians, pastors, and
biblical counselors, minister to those people God's way
who carry a psychological or psychiatric label. What is
that way? In this book, I lay out what I believe is God's
way, and I give a biblical rationale for how I arrived at
my conclusions.

When I was an unbeliever, my worldview was horizontally focused—on myself—for my own gain. I perceived
my life through my senses and by my own reasoning.[3]

---

3   The term *life* is often misunderstood and misused. The term is often used to
indicate that which "just happens." Rather, *life* refers to God's providence: His
most holy, wise, good, powerful, and purposeful sustaining and governing all of
His creatures and their actions. This is God's world and He is active in it. Praise

You could not have convinced me that there existed a far superior way of evaluating and responding to situations and other people. I practiced medicine as an unbeliever both at the university level (I held a faculty position) and in private practice for some three decades. All the while, I considered myself a scientist. However, I was uneasy about myself and my reasons for doing what I did. I now know that I was the problem. When I became a believer, some things changed, but not my practice of medicine. Patients were still problems to be solved, and applied biblical truth had no role in my approach to patient care and problem solving. It was easy for me to accept the Medical Model and psychological axioms to "explain" people and their problems. I, too, was led by feelings, experience, and human reason, apart from biblical truth.[4]

A second radical change occurred when I was introduced to biblical counseling as a way of life, not only for others, but for *me*. Not only did I begin to change individually, but I changed my view of medicine and how I practiced. I am growing in my understanding of biblical truth and its application in my life and in the lives of those that God brings to me. Now, I practice medicine in a way similar to how I counsel. I ask questions from

God! Acknowledging and acting upon this non-negotiable fact is especially critical for people who carry psychiatric labels.

4   Jay E. Adams, *The Power of Error* (Grand Rapids, MI: Baker, 1978). This interesting booklet speaks for itself.

the inside out (footnote 10). I minister to the whole person to the degree that I am able in the context of the person's physical complaints. I spell out the results of my change process, with how-tos, in greater detail in two of my books, *Being Christian in Your Medical Practice* and *True Competence in Medicine: Practicing Biblically-Based Medicine in a Fallen World*. This present book is a culmination of my thoughts based on my understanding of biblical truth as applied to the practice of medicine, especially in regard to people who have psychiatric labels. I hope to stimulate your thinking and move you to a radically different perspective, where you will regard feeling states as whole-person problems. The concept of whole person as I define it on page 18 is a biblical one. It contrasts with the term "holistic" which divides man into many compartments and emphasizes the "spiritual" in place of the Holy Spirit. My prayer is that all Christian physicians, pastors, and biblical counselors develop and nourish a heart for God's people, God's way, for His glory in the context of physical complaints.

The Necessity of a Proper Biblical Anthropology

In order to accomplish the goal of properly ministering to people with psychiatric labels, we must have a proper understanding of anthropology. God created man and placed him in His world. Both pre- and post-Fall, God had, and has, something to say about man: about what man thinks, desires, and does in relation to God and others. Jesus's summary of man's major duty post-Fall also applied to Adam pre-Fall: "love the Lord your God and love others with all of yourself" (Matt. 22:37–40 paraphrased).

There is only one place to discover God's view of man and how he should respond to God's providential ordering of life—in His Word (2 Tim. 3:15–17; 2 Pet. 1:3–4; Isa. 8:20). In this section, I address four aspects of man and close with a discussion of symptoms and signs:

- Man is a whole person who thinks, desires, and acts according to a standard and a set of presuppositions.

- Man is a duplex being: body, or outer man; and soul, or inner man.
- Man, as a whole person, is the image of God. As God's image-bearer, man thinks, desires, and acts/wills. These activities are both inner-man and outer-man activities.
- Man is a sensual being who is also a faith-based being.

Man is a Whole Person

The concept that man is a whole person is not new. Theologians throughout the ages have taught that man has an intellect (he thinks), affections (he desires), and volition (he acts). The concept of the whole person and its importance in biblical counseling is partially captured in question number 5 of the NANC Case Report Form (NANC is now ACBC, the Association of Certified Biblical Counselors): *What unbiblical habits of thinking and/or behaving are you seeing in the counselee (pre-conditioning)?*

Also, man is a duplex being (inner and outer man) and an image bearer of God. As such, man exists because God is. Man, a religious, worshipping being, is always in either proper *or* improper relationship to God. God thinks, man thinks—he is a rational being. God desires, man desires. God acts, man acts. Initially man thought, desired, and acted according to God's thoughts and ways. Post-Fall, man did not lose his personhood. He continues to think, desire, and act. These whole-person activities occur in *both* the inner and outer man.

The concept of man as a whole person is preeminently significant in the areas of salvation and sanctification. Therefore, a proper view of anthropology, salvation, and sanctification is of utmost importance for the physician in his practice of medicine, for the patient as he receives medical care, and for the pastor/biblical counselor and the counselee. Salvation is one hundred percent the work of God in the whole person. Man contributes nothing. He is wholly passive in the Holy Spirit's act of regeneration. At salvation, man is changed as a whole person from the inside-out by the work of the Holy Spirit. Man's wicked heart (heart of stone) is removed and replaced by one that is responsive to biblical truth (John 3:3–8; Ezek. 36:25–27). The gospel call is one of repentance and belief: "The time has come," Jesus said. "The kingdom of God is near. Repent and believe the good news" (Mark 1:15). The good news of the gospel implies pre-existing bad news.

Man responds to God's call as a result of God's work in man's heart (John 6:35, 44–45). Conversion consists of repentance and saving faith. Repentance and faith are the result of the full-orbed transformation of the *whole person* that theologians and the Bible term "the new birth": i.e., regeneration. After regeneration, the following changes occur in the believer:[5]

5   G. I. Williamson, *The Westminster Confession of Faith for Study Classes*, pages 97–98. I am referring to Williamson's schematic pictured on page 97 and his discussion throughout the chapter.

The believer has new *knowledge*. He thinks differently about himself—he knows his lost condition (Rom. 3:9–20). He thinks differently about God—he knows the divine remedy (John 3:16–21; Rom. 10:13–17). Man's mind is renewed.

The believer's *affections* are changed. He has a broken and contrite heart and a desire for intimacy with Christ through union with Him by the work of the Holy Spirit (2 Cor. 7:10–11; 1 Thess. 2:13). Man's "wanter" is changed; he desires differently.

The believer does something: he relies on Christ and His Word through the Holy Spirit (Acts 16:31; Phil. 3:7–11), he *willfully turns* from his previous manner of thinking, desiring, and acting. Man's will is changed. He acts differently.

As a result of salvation, the believer has a new motivation center: "Above all, guard your heart, for it is the wellspring of life" (Prov. 4:23). The believer has a new "thinker" with the capacity to think God's thoughts. He has a new "wanter" with the capacity to know and desire what God desires as given in His Word. He has the capacity to act as a child of God. He is changed as a *whole person.*

Progressive sanctification is the work of God's free grace. Salvation is one hundred percent God's work: man contributes nothing. On the other hand, sanctification is one hundred percent God's work AND one hundred percent man's work. Man's response is a whole-person response as a result of God's work both in *and* for him. Progressive sanctification is a continuous process whereby man increasingly brings his thoughts, desires, and actions in line with biblical truth (Phil. 2:12–13).

Life in Satan's kingdom and family is characterized by a return to man's post–Fall state. Adam, *desiring* to be like God and seeking a better life, willfully chose to do things his way, *thinking* that life would be better. Adam chose to be in competition with God. At salvation, man is placed in God's kingdom and family. Consequently, there is a radical change in the believer's thinking, desiring, and acting. In progressive sanctification, the believer will increasingly become more like Christ as a whole person. In place of living by his feelings (a "me-first" life directed by "I want" and "I deserve" and the person's own set of rules for his benefit), the believer is motivated and directed by biblical principles through the work of the Holy Spirit. Generally, changed feelings follow. But even if they don't, the believer is more concerned with pleasing God than with having good feelings.

The believer's goal, as a restored image bearer of God, is growth in the likeness of Christ (2 Cor. 5:9). A new pattern of God-pleasing replaces a self-pleasing motivation learned as a member of Satan's kingdom and family. The believer increasingly replaces thoughts and desires that are anti-God and pro-self with thoughts, desires, and actions that please God.

Man is a Duplex Being

The Bible's view of man begins at creation. Man was created by God. From nothing, something came. Man was created a duplex unit. He was created a material being out of the dust of the ground (Gen. 2:7). Adam was formed out of the dust of the ground, but it was only when the breath of life was breathed into him that he became a living soul/being. The uniqueness of man was not in him being a living soul (Gen. 1:20, 21, 24, 30; 2:19), but in the manner in which God brought about that result. God's personal, direct in-breathing was a separate act on God's part, which distinguished man from animals.

As a duplex unit, man is outer man: a physical being (the material aspect of man), and he is inner man: a spiritual being. Man has a body but he is not only physical. He has an inner man but he is not only spiritual. Because of man's duplexity, his outer and inner man are linked (Matt. 10:28; James 2:26; Eccles. 3:21; 12:7). Each influences the other. Because man is a whole person, what he thinks and wants—both inner and outer-man activities—affect how and what he feels. In turn, thinking and wanting determine the person's feelings and his response to his situation and ultimately his response to God. Inner-man activities such as guilt, deception, and denial, or gratitude and joy affect how one feels and functions. Bodily problems can influence (not *cause*) how and what a person thinks, desires, and does. Both Elijah (1 Kings 18–19) and David (Psalms 32 and 38) had outer and inner-man consequences. The consequence of Elijah's extreme physical activity and lack of rest had an influence on his inner-man function. David's unconfessed sin produced both inner-man and outer-man turmoil.

The Bible uses various terms to describe the inner man and its function and its relationship to the body. These terms include *heart*, *mind*, *spirit*, *soul*, *will*, and *conscience*. Briefly, and for clarification, *heart* is the usual term used in Bible for the inner man. It is the person known wholly to God, hidden and known partially to himself, and unknown to others. What is in a person's heart is displayed in and by his thoughts, desires, and actions; the heart is often equated with the inner man.

Soul and *spirit* are terms used to designate the inner man in relation *to* the body and *out* of relation to body, respectively. *Will* is the volitional aspect of the inner man that is expressed via activity: both inner- and outer-man activity. I add inner-man activity because of Christ's teaching in passages such as Matthew 5:22–23, 27–29. *Mind* is sometimes equated with *heart*, especially in terms of function. It is the site of man's rational and thinking capacities. The *conscience* is the judging-accusing-excusing aspect of the inner man, based on a standard.

Biblically speaking, man thinks, hopes, fears, purposes, doubts, considers, and decides courses of action in his inner man. Patterns of thinking, desiring, and actions are formed in the heart and flow from it. The heart is the site of man's motivational and belief systems. It is where the Holy Spirit initially operates in regeneration and continually resides in the believer, illumining and enlightening him (1 Cor. 2:1–5, 14–15; 4:6; Eph. 1:14, 17–18; 1 Thess. 1:5–6; 1 John 2:20, 27). Opening man's blind eyes and softening his hard heart is a work of God. It begins at regeneration and continues throughout progressive sanctification. As a result, man understands, begins to apply biblical truth, and grows as a God-pleaser, increasingly putting off self-pleasing in its many forms.

Inner-man activities may be invisible to others and known only to the performer. For instance, in Matthew 5:21–22, 27–29, Jesus pictures murder and adultery as an in-the-heart activity which may or may not be expressed in overt physical actions. "You have heard that it was said to the people long ago, 'Do not murder,' and anyone who murders will be subject to judgment. But I tell you that anyone who is angry with his brother will be subject to judgment. Again, anyone who says to his brother, 'Raca' is answerable to the Sanhedrin. But anyone who says, 'You fool' will be in danger of the fire of hell. . . . You have heard it said, 'Do not commit adultery.' But I tell you that anyone who looks at a woman lustfully has already committed with her in his heart."

The Bible teaches that man lives out of his heart—man's active heart is expressed in the context of many different situations (Matt. 12:33–36; 15:16–20; Mark 7:18–20; Luke 6:43–45; Prov. 4:23). Man is an inside-out person with root (motivation) and fruit (thoughts, desires, and actions).

The Bible does not view man's behavior as isolated and unrelated to his inner person or his situation. Rather, man is a whole person who thinks, desires, and acts in both his inner and outer man. Man, as a duplex being, thinks and desires (some would say *emotes*) in *both* his brain and his inner man. Anatomically, the brain is divided into lobes. The cerebral cortex and frontal-parietal lobes are said to be the thinking part of the brain, where judgment and logical reasoning reside. The cortex is the strategy center of the brain. The emotional center of the brain is the limbic system, what I call the affective center of the brain. Feelings and emotions are linked to thoughts and desires, and are inner and outer-man activities. Emotions (however defined) and feelings are not the same. People tend to equate the two and thereby divest feeling-states from thinking and wanting/desires. Rather, thinking and desires, with or without actions, are the issue in all feeling states; it is the whole person that must be addressed. (Later in the book, I make a distinction between feelings and emotions anatomically and theologically).

The functional capacity of the inner man (root) and its expression (fruit) can be compared to a sponge or pitcher (heart) filled with some substance (contents of the heart). The illustration is not perfect because of the active nature of man's heart. But the principle is true: only what is inside will come out. That which is inside comes out when the sponge is squeezed or the pitcher is tipped over. The squeezing and tipping represents pressure (problems and unpleasantness in life) that occurs because of God's providential control. The person's circumstances are the *context*, not the cause, of the outpouring of his inner man, including bad-feeling states such as depression. When the *source* of bad feelings are the result of wanting and thinking that is not Holy Spirit-directed and biblically-based, or when a person *responds* to bad feelings in an unbiblical manner, there is sin. The term *sin* seems to be used infrequently today, even in biblical counseling. The trend seems to be especially prevalent in the area of psychological labels (i.e., feeling states) and the people who have received them.

Man is the Image of God

When discussing the topic of man as God's image, common questions include the following: "What is the image?" and "Which part of man is the image?" The image is the whole person. It is all of man: his thoughts, desires or affections, and actions. According to Ephesians 4:24, Col. 3:10, 2 Cor. 3:18, and Rom. 8:29, the believer, as a whole person, is re-created in the image of God:

- In knowledge—he is to be a truth-thinker and truth-teller to himself, to others, and preeminently, to God.
- In holiness—he is to consecrate himself in thought and desire to pleasing God.
- In righteousness—he is to be willfully obedient; his acts are to please God.

Initially, pre-Fall man correctly received and reevaluated God's initial revelation about God, man, and creation. Man took in information—facts—through his senses and rightly processed them because he had a proper interpretive grid: God's directly revealed Word. Man's whole person—inner and outer man—was unaffected by sin. He was able to think God's thoughts and desire what pleased God. He was able to function as a God-pleaser. However, Adam, in God's perfect world and in proper relationship to God and creation, accepted Satan's invitation to "be like God knowing good and evil" (Gen. 3:5). Subsequently, irrationality and self-pleasing reigned: "But whoever fails to find me harms himself; all who hate me love death" (Prov. 8:36). As a result of Adam's *first* sin, in judgment God cursed Satan and Adam's and Eve's present and future activities. Instantly, Adam was guilty and lost original righteousness and his right relationship to God. He was God's enemy. He was spiritually dead. He no longer thought God's thoughts, desired God's desires, or obeyed God willingly and lovingly. Adam now had a new mindset and a new lifestyle. As a self-pleaser, he was now interested in only getting; he was motivated by "I want" and "I deserve." Adam now wrongly interpreted himself, God and His revelation, creation, and others. Misery and chaos soon filled the earth, as well as Adam's heart (Rom. 5:12–14).

After the Fall, Adam and all men interpreted facts (please note: all facts are interpreted) following autonomous human reasoning—*unaided* by Scripture and the illumination of the Holy Spirit. This is one expression of suppressing the truth in unrighteousness (Rom. 1:18–20). Reason and motivation were not guided by biblical truth. Such is the result of the noetic effect of sin.[6] Post-Fall, man continues to be a sensual being but his thoughts and desires are unchecked by biblical truth: totally in the unbeliever and far too frequently in the believer. The believer continues, in varying degrees, to function according to his feelings and wants, resulting in feeling-directed behavior.[7]

The following schematic pictures the connection between thoughts, desires, actions, and feelings:

General

---

6   *Noetic* refers to the effect of sin on thoughts and thinking. The effects of sin are prevalent in every area of life. Biblically-controlled thinking (and wanting) is God's gracious corrective for the believer with his changed inner-man.

7   Feeling-directed behavior (suprasensual living) is one manifestation of suppressing the truth of God (Rom. 1:18–23). Unbelievers live in darkness and love it (John 3:16–21; Proverbs 4:18–19). For the unbeliever, self is always on the throne in principle and often in practice, though expressed visibly in varying degrees and ways. He does not always visibly demonstrate the utter wickedness of his heart. Functionally, God has no place in the unbeliever's life. Sadly, the believer, because of his prior membership in Satan's family and kingdom, often functions as if God has no place in his life. This truth may seem strange to believers, but it is the reality of remaining corruption and the resultant habituation of self-pleasing (footnotes 8, 10, 12, 25, 35–37).

Pre-situational thinking, wanting, and responding→ present situation→ whole-person response (thinking, wanting, and behavior)→ possible physiological changes in the body including the cardiopulmonary systems, gastrointestinal system, the skin, the musculoskeletal system, and the release of various neurotransmitters, and other chemicals → signs and symptoms→ function

Biblical

Pre-situational thinking, wanting, and responding→ present situation→ whole-person response characterized by *biblical* thinking and wanting→ God-honoring response as a whole person with or without physiological symptoms and/or signs→ God-pleasing function to the degree that the person is physically able

Unbiblical

Pre-situational thinking, wanting, and responding→ present situation→ whole-person response characterized by *unbiblical* thinking and wanting→ possible physiological changes such as a rapid heart and respiratory rate, diarrhea, abdominal pain, sweating headache, fatigue, and pain→ unbiblical response in terms of action→ bad feelings→ decreased physical function→ patterned thinking, wanting, and doing, which may be cyclical

Man is a Physical, Sensual, Faith-Based Being

By God's creative design, man is a physical, sensual, and faith-based being.[8] Because he is a whole person, there is an *affective* aspect to man's being—he desires. Feelings (which are not synonymous with desires or emotions) are part of man's make-up.[9] However, man is not his feelings or his emotions (however defined), although he often functions as if he is. In fact, emotions and feelings are linked to thoughts, desires, wants, and actions/behavior. This link—thinking, wanting, doing, and feeling—describes man's whole-person activity as a child of God or of Satan. Sadly, even believers sometimes function as they did when in Satan's family and kingdom.

Often, feelings and emotions are equated. Physiologically and anatomically, they are not the same. Feelings, such as pain and pruritis (itch), are associated with specific neural pathways, which can be manipulated in an effort to decrease the sensation. On the other hand,

8   Man was created a theologian and continues so after the Fall. He lives in or out of a proper relationship to God. As such, man is a revelation receiver, interpreter, and implementer. Everyone gathers information through his senses—he hears, sees, touches/feels, tastes, and smells. He evaluates that information in his brain and in his heart (man is a thinking being, both in the outer and inner man). In the book, I contrast sensual living with suprasensual living (footnotes 7, 25, 35-37). The Bible calls on believers to put off sensual living: that directed by the senses, unaided by biblical truth. They are to put on suprasensual living: "seeing" God's providence through the eyes of saving faith and biblical truth (2 Cor. 5:7).

9   D. Powlison, "What Do You Feel," *Journal of Pastoral Practice 10,* (1992): 50–61.

while accepting anger as an emotion, you will not find in the body a neural-anger circuit. Neither will you find a neural-depression or neural-worry circuit. Angry people can demonstrate physical changes (a red face, rapid pulse, and increased sweating), which are conveyed through the autonomic nervous system. Moreover, both feelings and emotions have a cognitive component: thoughts and desires influence feelings (such as pain) and emotions, *however defined*. Understanding the link between thoughts and desires and feelings is critical in helping people with psychiatric labels. Most publications from both the medical and counseling worlds that address feeling-states lack a definition for *emotion*, and equate feelings with emotions. I agree that feelings/emotions both have a cognitive and affective aspect.

Man was created a faith-based creature. By that I mean man reasons and believes according to a standard. His standard will be his feelings, his experience, or his own reasoning in contrast to the Word of God rightly understood and applied. The use of the first three reasons are one hallmark of sensual living in contrast to and opposed to suprasensual living (see footnotes 7, 9, 25, 35–37). Man's source of faith may be either science as he defines it or a person, including his own decision to decide his standard. His faith has an object—he has faith in something—and a goal. His faith takes him somewhere—it helps him accomplish his goal. Two pertinent questions arise: What is the object of the person's faith?

And what is its source? Remember that I have said that the issue of control and its lack, *and* resources and their lack, lie at the heart of depression (as well as fear, anger, and worry). Only the believer can rightly interpret circumstances as God's providence. Once he does, he turns his attention to the God of his circumstances. Such was the case with Jane.

Our culture has equated feelings with thinking, but less so thinking with desires. For example, a person may ask you how you *feel* about something. The person may be asking you to emote, but generally he is inquiring about your *thinking*. He misses the crucial connection between thoughts and desires as heart-motivated, and their role in the generation of *and* response to feelings. Patients and counselees who carry psychiatric labels rarely talk about thinking and desires or wants. Nor do they speak about good feelings. Rather, they complain of bad feelings and their expectation, and even demand, for relief. They wrongly focus on the presence of feelings rather than on their source and the proper response to them.

Symptoms and Signs: An Important Aspect for Understanding Feelings States

When considering the duplexity of man it is important, even mandatory, to distinguish between symptoms and signs. Following the Medical Model, the presence of symptoms and/or signs is explained by genes, biology, molecule, biochemistry, neurotransmitters, etc. The Medical Model of disease excludes the person's relationship with Christ and the indwelling Holy Spirit. Regrettably, following the Medical Model, these latter two facts are often denied or considered improperly by the Christian physician, pastor, and the biblical counselor (as well as the counselee and patient).

A s*ymptom* is subjective. There is nothing to measure. The amount and degree of a symptom rests solely on the person's report. A *sign* is objective and can be measured. It can be quantified by some instrument other than self report. For instance, fever is a sign with or without symptoms and is measured by a tool (thermometer). Feverishness is a symptom that is not measurable by any objective tool.

Another helpful concept in understanding feeling states is the difference between something wrong *with* the body and *in* the body. Take the example of a patient-reported rapid heart rate (tachycardia). Patients may feel that their heart is racing or skipping (the sensation is termed *palpitations*). When measured, the heart rate and rhythm may be normal. The sensation that the patient feels is a symptom. In most cases, there is no problem *with* the body. On the other hand, a measured, rapid heart rate is a sign. At times, the person may not be aware of his tachycardia. Physician and patient alike need to determine if the problem is *with* or *in* the body. A rapid heart rate may be due to a normally functioning heart generated by whole-person activities such as fear or anger or by physical exertion—especially in a de-conditioned person. These are examples of something wrong *in* the body. For clarification, tachycardia in a fit person doing strenuous work or activity is a normal physiological response: there is nothing wrong with the body or the heart.

Examples of something wrong *with* the body include tachycardia due to anemia, pneumonia, a hyperactive thyroid, or blood clots to the lung (pulmonary emboli). Even though the heart is not the problem (it is working as God intended) the increased heart rate is a response to a pathological condition within the body. There is something wrong with the body but not necessarily the heart. Another example of something wrong *with* the body is a rapid heart rate due to a damaged heart, from whatever cause.

Thoughts Regarding Feeling States

It is time to apply the previously discussed biblical anthropological facts to feeling states. As I have said, I consider bad-feeling states (so-called psychological and mental health disorders) such as worry (often the worrier is labeled as having an *anxiety disorder*), fear (often the fearful person is labeled as having a *panic attack*), anger (often the angry person is labeled as having an *anger disorder*), and depression (the person is labeled as having a *depressive disorder)* as whole-person problems. These bad-feeling states are the result of unbiblical thinking and wanting about God, self, others, and circumstances at the moment, and often as a patterned lifestyle. They spring from root, or heart, issues. Fear, worry, anger, and depression are feeling-directed reactions to circumstances, people, and ultimately to God. Each one has a source that is within the person. According to the Bible, worry is always sinful. There is no way to worry in a biblical manner. On the other hand, there is a biblical way to fear (Prov. 1:7) and to be angry (Eph. 4:26). Fear of the Lord is always biblical. Fear springing from a desire to please God and to be a good steward of one's body is always godly. Self-serving anger is always sinful.

The questions before us, which I will answer, are these: Is it a godly response to situations to become depressed? (However defined.) Is there such a thing as "godly depression"? Is depression sinful?

For clarity, I am not saying that people don't feel. Nor am I saying that bad-feeling states don't exist. Nor am I saying that all bad feelings are necessarily the result of personal and particular sin. *But they may be.*

Strikingly, the link between thoughts, desires, and feeling-generated actions and more feelings is quite apparent when I talk to patients and counselees. When questioned according to biblical data-gathering principles, the person invariably associates his feeling state with two main elements: his thinking and wanting about *control* and *resources*, and his perceived lack of both.[10]

---

10   By "biblical data gathering," I mean asking appropriate questions that address root and fruit issues. Questions are intended to learn the person's beliefs and attitudes that motivate and drive behavior and actions. Questions are designed to link feelings with thinking, wanting, and doing, which are whole-person activities. See *Tactics* by Gregory Koukl: the book is a guide to having better conversations regarding Christian truth and their application in life. He makes a case for listening and asking questions, both of which are vital in the counseling/discipling setting. (Gregory Koukl, *Tactics: A Game Plan for Discussing Your Christian Convictions* (Grand Rapids, MI: Zondervan, 2009).

Again, I reiterate that "feeling bad" and "bad feelings" are *not* necessarily the result of sinful thinking and wanting. But they may be (James 5:14–16; Psalm 32, 38). On the other hand, not every unbiblical response to others and circumstances necessarily leads to bad feelings. For instance, a person may become bitter and resentful toward a spouse or co-worker, yet not feel bad about this. But a patterned lifestyle characterized by unbiblical responses to God's providence (what people term "life") has consequences (Prov. 13:15; Gal. 6:7–9).

We are sensual, physical beings by God's design and our bodies are failing. As a result, bad feelings are part of man's earthly existence (Rom. 5:12–14; 2 Cor. 4:16–18). Therefore, a person with bad feelings should not be given a psychological label or be diagnosed with a mental illness. Rather, the *source* of these feelings and the person's *response* to them should be evaluated in terms of the person's wanting and thinking. Unfortunately, by following the Medical Model of disease, even if the *source* of a person's bad feelings are sin-engendered, even if a person *reacts* wrongly to his bad feelings, and even if they *persist* in that wrong response, they may well be labeled as having a mental illness.[11]

In order to properly evaluate feeling states, the following truths need to be correctly understood and applied:

- Whole-person activities of thinking, wanting, and doing

---

11   See footnote 2.

occur in both the inner and outer man. Feelings are produced as a result of these whole-person activities. As such, inner-man activities affect the outer man and vice versa.

- Man is a duplex being, both inner man (heart) and outer man (his body including the brain).

- People who are diagnosed with a bad-feeling state characterized by fear, worry, anger, or depression generally believe that something outside of them *makes* them feel a certain way: bad. People might label this phenomenon as *stress*. They fail to link *reactive* feelings to their thoughts and desires. These feelings control their interpretation of and reaction to circumstances. They consider themselves victims to that which is outside of them. In other words, they function as if their life circumstances are God's fault: He let them down.

- A person can manipulate or change their circumstances, or they can take medications, which may blunt their bad feelings. But neither activity gets to the root of the matter—the person's motivation, which includes thinking and wanting about himself or herself, others, and God.

- Biblically speaking, the whole person is involved in every feeling state, whether the feelings are good or bad.

Questions to Answer and Points to Ponder

What is depression? Is it sin? In one or two sentences, please include

- your knee-jerk reaction to the question and the reasons for your answer;
- your definition of depression;
- how you arrived at your definition.

When speaking of depression, generally described as bad feelings and behavior that accompanies or follows those feelings, what comes to mind? As you answer this question, consider the following:

- Where do you go to find information about depression?
- What is your bias about depression (everyone presupposes some belief and acts upon it)?
- What standard do you use in *giving* and *accepting* the label of depression?
- What standard do you use for *responding* to a person with that label?
- What place does biblical truth have in *helping* people with that label?
- How do you *define* help and what is your *standard* for defining it?

These questions need answers. This book is designed to help Christian physicians, pastors, and biblical counselors answer them and function as God's kind of people, doctors, and counselors. A corollary purpose of this book is to help all Christians rightly understand and address bad-feeling states, especially depression.

A Proper Starting Point Requires a Correct Definition

For any endeavor, one must begin at the beginning. In addressing feeling states, what is your starting point and your rationale for it? It is my contention that, too often, believer and unbeliever alike begin with the secular definition of depression. Consequently, the diagnosis of depression and all the attached baggage is carried over to the person, patient, and counselee. Many assumptions are likely to be made without gathering appropriate data regarding the person—his thoughts, his desires, and his actions, and their role in the production of his feelings. Because the person is a whole person, a duplex being, and an image bearer of God, data-gathering questions should bring to light the person's hopes, expectations, wants, and demands that may be unbiblical and/or unfulfilled.

Depression (and any feeling state), however defined, is always associated with thinking and wanting in the context of some situation. No person enters into a circumstance *de novo*, because every human being is, functionally, a theologian. By this, I mean that every human being brings certain thoughts and desires about themselves and God to every situation they encounter (remember, terms such as "life" and "situation" refer to God's providence). Especially for the depressed person, their functional view of God is determined by the triad of their feelings, their experience, and their own reasoning. These, rather than biblical principles and a Holy Spirit-directed desire to please God, govern their responses to situations. People labeled as depressed interpret God and themselves through their circumstances; they often have a distorted view of God and reality. God seems so far away, hidden, or not there. They perceive God as very small, and His presence as burdensome.

Such people consider and label themselves *unfulfilled* and *resourceless*. They *feel* caught in a black hole, having no resources to enable them to escape. Their hole looks so deep and their mountain seems so high. Their feelings and the desire, even demand, for relief become powerful motivating forces. But if these people are believers, they are living a lie, because they are functioning as if the ever-present God is uncaring, impotent, or both. They label themselves helpless and hopeless, and act accordingly.[12] Their thoughts and desires are focused on their circumstances. Their response is often a learned and practiced behavior linked to thoughts and desires,

---

12   Everyone lives out of and in concert with an identity, either self-generated or others-generated. It seems that our culture is enamored with labels and identities. No matter the source (self or others), the person, motivated by the label, sets an agenda for himself. He pursues the agenda sometimes relentlessly. Jesus knew who He was, what His mission was, and His Father. He resolutely set His face toward Jerusalem (Luke 9:51). Others may lose sight of who they are in Christ and their resources in Him and the Holy Spirit. As a result, they label themselves as resourceless, hopeless, and helpless. They function accordingly. Labels do matter.

all of which are expressed as "bad feelings." The label of helpless and hopeless, the person's feelings, and the inordinate desire to have relief, all determine and control their thinking and wanting; feelings and actions follow. The reverse is true as well: feelings and action influence thoughts and desires. For example, the Bible teaches that if you do right, you will think right (Gen. 4:7). Often, the person's life becomes a self-perpetuating cycle of feeling-oriented thinking and feeling-directed behavior.

In contrast to the *Diagnostic and Statistical Manual of Mental Disorders* (DSM), you will not find terms such as *mental illness* or *depressive disorders* in the Bible. But you do find a myriad of words that describe an individual's feeling states in the context of whole-person activities: thoughts, desires, and actions. Biblical terms include

- downcast (Gen. 4:5–6; Ps. 42:5–6,11; 43:5; 1 Sam. 1:18),
- downhearted (1 Sam. 1:8),
- cast down (Lam. 3:19–20),
- weighed down (Prov. 12:25),
- distress (Ps. 25:17; Jer. 4:31; 48:41; 49:22).

There is a Third Way

What is your starting point? You will either accept the culture's definition of depression and give care based on the Medical Model of disease, or you will begin with the person and use biblical principles to help him replace living by feelings and experience with living by the Word of God. If you choose the latter, I would consider that progress.

Yet there is a better way. I began to address this third way under the section "Symptoms and Signs." Based on who man is by God's creative design—a whole person, duplex being, the image of God—we can and should consider depression in the same light as worry and fear. God in His Word makes clear that worry is sin (Matt. 6:24–34; Phil. 4:6–9). In regards to fear, we are told to fear the Lord (Prov. 1:7; 2:5; 8:13; 9:10; Ps. 111:10). We are told not to fear circumstances and uncertainty (Isa. 41:10, 13; 43:1,5; 44:6–8), men and their reproaches (Isa. 51:7, 12; Matt. 10:26, 28, 31), or disgrace (Isa. 54:4).[13]

---

13   The book of Isaiah gives emphasis to the subject of fear. God sent Isaiah to Israel to bring his charge of faithlessness and rebellion against them (Isa. 1:2–3; 31:1–3; 57:3–10). He also calls on the godly to seek the Lord: the book contains a message of hope. It is in the midst of turmoil, both physical and spiritual, that Isaiah calls for individuals and the nation not to fear: 7:3–4 (Ahaz and the people shook with fear); 8:11–13 (a contrast between two fears: fear of man and circumstances and fear of the Lord); 10:24 (a word of encouragement to the remnant in Judah); 35:4 (those with fearful/anxious hearts: inner-man angst); 37:6 (to Hezekiah's emissaries at the time of Assyria's threat); 51:17 (the reproach to those with God's law in their hearts). Consider the terms self-preservation and self-protection. Protecting self can be a matter of good stewardship. Proverbs 19:2 teaches: it is not good to have zeal without knowledge or to be hasty. Proverbs 22:3 teaches: a prudent man sees danger and takes refuge. These two proverbs teach that wisdom and prudence rather than a physiological flight-or-fight response help believers to fear God's way.

Moreover, we are told to trust and love God even when we are tempted to be sinfully fearful (Ps. 56:3–4; 1 John 4:18). Based on biblical truth, we can and should agree that terms such as "social anxiety disorder" and "panic attack" are euphemisms for sin. Those labels dishonor God by undermining the clarity, authority, necessity, and sufficiency of His Word. The labels do not help the Christian caught up in the whole-person activity described by that label. The label incorrectly explains what is going on in the whole person.

The same conclusion can and should be drawn in regard to those labeled as having a depressive disorder. I base this conclusion on the following:

- When the cultural definitions of *depression* are imposed on the Bible (as when fear and worry are classified as a "panic attack" or "social anxiety disorder"), the Bible will not be used to address the whole person, *or* the Bible will be used in ways that God did not intend, including helping the person feel better. Good feelings may, and often do, come from pleasing God, but seeking them can never be the primary reason for pleasing God.

- Depression should be defined as a whole-person activity of thoughts, desires, wants, and actions in which the person gives in to feelings and gives up on some, many, or all of his responsibilities, and ultimately on God.

You may ask: What gives you the right to define depression? My answer is: Why shouldn't I? As I noted in my introduction, I long functioned under the authority of the Medical Model, the Biopsychosocial Model, and the Biopsychosocialspiritual Model of disease in lieu of the authority of Scripture. Biblical principles had no place in the practice of medicine, I thought. My concern is that the Christian community will continue to begin with secular definitions and thus import secular assumptions to the person and to the Bible. In contrast, the biblically-based pastor, physician and counselor are armed with the construct that man is a whole person, a duplex being who thinks, desires, and wills/acts in both the inner and outer man. As a *helper* and *comforter* of the person with bad feelings (whether friend, doctor, or counselor), the helper is free and obligated to whole-heartedly and unreservedly rely on the Word of God. The issue of how to do this (the methodology) is the subject for another time.

However, we must agree on the principle of bringing the truth of God to bear on people—patients and counselees—in order to help motivate them to change their thoughts, desires, and actions. Changed feelings may follow. But simply feeling better should not be the goal of the Christian. Rather, pleasing God—in their thinking, desires, and actions—is to be the primary goal of the Christian. As 2 Corinthians 5:9 says, "So we make it our goal to please him, whether we are at home in the body or away from it." The above principle has far-reaching implications.

The Requirement of a Proper Scriptural Starting Point

A proper starting point is essential for developing a proper biblical perspective regarding bad-feeling states. My starting point, and I hope yours, is the Bible, rightly understood and applied. When faced with a person labeled as having depression (or being depressed: notice the noun-verb interface), do you begin with the Bible? Do you apply its truth to the whole person—their thoughts, desires, actions, and feelings? If you do, how do you use your Bible? As you find feeling-based words in the Bible, do you import your culture's definition to them? Do you accept the culture's worldview, forcing it on the Bible in an attempt to help hurting people?[14]

---

14 The following criteria for the diagnosis of depression are from the DSM-IV. The DSM is considered psychiatry's "Bible." However, some researchers argue that the newly proposed definition of depression in the DSM-V, which includes "grief after the loss of a loved one," is opening the door for a false-positive diagnosis of depression and the unnecessary treatment of people who are "simply going through the *normal* process of grieving." The terms "normal process of grief" and "grief process" are loaded ones

Both secular and biblical approaches are purported to help hurting people. There are now two definitions that must be agreed upon: that of *depression* and that of *help.* The two are linked.

---

and require biblical verification before they are accepted and acted upon. I address this issue in my book: *Joy and Grief: God's Answer for Hard Times* (Greenville, SC: Ambassador, 2012). According to the DSM-IV, a diagnosis of depression requires at least five of the nine following symptoms to be present for at least two weeks:

1. Depressed mood most of the day, nearly every day.

2. Markedly diminished interest or pleasure in all or almost all activities (anhedonia).

3. Significant weight loss when not dieting, or weight gain, or decrease or increase in appetite nearly every day.

4. Insomnia or sleeping too much nearly every day.

5. Psychomotor agitation or retardation nearly every day.

6. Fatigue or loss of energy nearly every day.

7. Feelings of worthlessness, or excessive or inappropriate guilt.

8. Diminished ability to think or concentrate, or indecisiveness.

9. Recurrent thoughts of death or recurrent suicidal ideation, or a suicide attempt or specific plan for committing suicide.

The criteria has been liberalized (both in the PHQ 9 and PHQ 2). The recent definition set forth by the US Preventive Services Task Force (USPSTF) is obtained by the answers to two questions:

> 1) Over the past 2 weeks, have you ever felt down, depressed, or hopeless?
>
> 2) Over the past 2 weeks, have you felt little pleasure or interest in doing things?

These questions and their respective answers are reported to have a sensitivity of 96 percent and specificity of 57 percent in regards to diagnosing depression.

It is increasingly evident to me that most Christians—lay people, church leaders, and physicians—have accepted the definition of depression provided by the secular, medical community. We live in a *feeling-ized* culture: people follow their own feelings and their own self-interest. An "I want" and "I deserve" mentality is center stage. When Christians follow the culture, they bring feeling-ized language into the Bible as a competing means to evaluate themselves and their situation. People reacting to circumstances based on the triad of feelings, experiences, and unaided human reasoning is one characteristic of a feeling-ized culture.

In contrast, Holy Spirit-directed application of biblical truth is God's antidote for a feeling-oriented and directed lifestyle. Biblical truth rightly presented and applied is necessary for people to change their thoughts and desires (which have morphed into wants). People have raised their desires to a status of "I deserve," and therefore they act accordingly. Galatians 5:16–18 depicts the believer's conflict between self-pleasing and God-pleasing:

> So I say live by the Spirit and you will not gratify the desires of the sinful nature. For the sinful nature desires what is contrary to the Spirit, and the Spirit what is contrary to the sinful nature. They are in conflict with each other, so that you do not do what you want. But if you are led by the Spirit, you are not under law.

Our culture has no monopoly on feeling-orientation. All cultures down through the ages have been driven by feelings. The Old and New Testaments provide ample evidence for this fact. The old nature, or old man—what the believer was as an unbeliever—consists of whole-person corruption, and the lifestyle and habit patterns of thoughts, desires, and actions developed as a member of Satan's kingdom and family. This corruption is radical and comprehensive. It is manifested, in varying degrees, as "me first," self-pleasing, and self-worshipping. Sadly, this habituation is carried over into the believer's life: habits die hard (Prov. 5:21–22; 22:6; 26:11–12). For the believer, there is a lingering appeal for the *vomit* spoken of in Proverbs 26:11. There is a whole-person conflict. In part, progressive sanctification is the process by which believers die to the appeal of the vomit (a desire for the previous lifestyle and all it offers in order to please self) and live to please God. The conflict is inside-out and is reflected in both the inner and outer man. It manifests itself as feeling-directed thinking, wanting, and acting in contrast to Holy-Spirit directed, biblically-controlled thinking, wanting, and acting (also see James 3:13–4:3 and Rom. 8:5–8, 9–11).

Conflict

As a result of accepting the definition provided by the medical and secular community, there is a conflict between biblical truth and its application, and the culture's approach and solution to all areas of life, including feeling states. I suspect that many biblical counselors, pastors, and Christian physicians would reject the above line of reasoning. It is easy to accept the prevalent rationale behind the medical diagnosis of depression. There are several reasons for this acceptance.

First, almost everyone has experienced or is acquainted with someone who has experienced bad feelings in varying degrees, generally expressed as despondency, sadness, discouragement, or extreme loneliness. These states may be termed *spiritual depression* (in contrast to *physical depression*). The assumption is that depression "just is." Depression is assumed to be part of life for both the believer and unbeliever, and its presence is assumed to have nothing to do with unbiblical thinking and wanting.

Second, there is an *after-the-fact* approach to feeling states. By this I mean the emphasis seems to be that biblical truth and its application is helpful only *after* the person has become depressed. Following the Medical Model, it is assumed that something is wrong *with* the body. Consequently, a body-mechanic approach to the person is most often used. In counseling, a spiritual-mechanic approach to the problem and person is often used as a means to produce good feelings. This approach may take several forms, such as preaching the gospel to yourself or reminding the person what he is in Christ. These truths have a place in helping people get victory, but we must ask the person several questions: What truths is he applying presently? What truths did he apply in the past? What are the results? Functionally, the person is dichotomized. The *source* of bad feelings *and* the person's *response* to them are considered a body problem. The whole person and man's duplex nature, both inner and outer man and their respective activities of thoughts, desires, and actions, are ignored.

Third, there is an emphasis on suffering and feelings, and the psalms are often quoted to support this emphasis. The point seems to be that depression (using the secular definition) just "happens to" the psalmist, Paul, and even Jesus. Therefore, it must not be sinful. A patterned way of thinking, wanting, and acting is usually not addressed. However, the following points are crucial to a proper understanding of suffering as depicted in the psalms:

1. One outstanding feature of the psalms is their Christological perspective. Jesus lived the psalms. He is the true Psalmist. Beginning with Psalm 1 and throughout the Psalter, Jesus is the man who did not walk, stand, or sit in the place of sinners. Yet on the cross, He went to hell in place of His people. He paid the penalty for their sins. Jesus had physical problems and bad feelings. As the God-man, via His humanity, He thought, desired, and acted as a whole person. Categorically, Jesus was *not* His feelings. He was led by the Word of God and the fullness of the Holy Spirit (Isa. 11:1–4; John 4:31–34; Matt. 4:1–11; Luke 4:1–13). He had one overriding desire: to please His Father

(John 4:31–34). He accurately modeled the biblical way of responding to the reality of hard times (see John Murray's booklet, *Behind God's Frowning Providence*).[15] Jesus's victory is every believer's victory. The psalms point us to Christ and His application of biblical truth. But one patient I was treating told me, "I am not Christ, so just give me relief." I agreed that she was not Christ, but as a believer she was re-created to become more *like* Christ. Part of the supernatural work of the Holy Spirit (regeneration) is to help motivate her to function as a God-pleaser in the midst of hard times. Bad feelings were part of Jesus's life, but they were never His guide. They did not originate from unbiblical thinking or wanting.[16] We would do well to remember the Holy Spirit's perspective when reading the psalms.

---

15   John Murray, *Behind A Frowning Providence*, (Carlisle, PA: Banner of Truth, 1990).

16   Here we are faced with the issue of Jesus' impeccability. Jesus did not sin and could not sin. It was impossible for Him to sin. This doctrine is taught in such places as Luke 1:35; John 8:46; 14:30; 2 Cor. 5:21; Heb. 4:15; 7:26; 9:14; 1 John 3:5. At the same time, the Bible echoes Hebrews 4:15 (*For we do not have a high priest who is unable to sympathize with our weaknesses, but we have one who has been tempted in every way just as we are—yet without sin*). Jesus understood and stepped into our human-ness: our human condition. But He was without sin in His nature and practice: He engaged in no sin and no sinning. Scripture represents Jesus as the ideal man realized: Heb. 2:8–9; 1 Cor. 15:45; 2 Cor. 3:18.

2. The feeling words so often used in the psalms—see at least Psalm 6, 13, 32, 38, 42–43, 73, 77—fit situations and emphasize a relational reference of the psalmist, both to God and to others. However, the situation and the surrounding details are often unknown. Rather, the psalmist's response to his situation is emphasized. Often there is a private engagement of the whole person from the inside out. The psalmist's response helps give the reader a gaze into the mind of Christ and points him to the true Psalmist. Jesus is also our High Priest, who has experienced the human condition to its fullest extent, yet without sin (2 Cor. 5:21; Heb. 4:14–16). His identification with us is to be followed by our identification with Him. Becoming more like Christ at least means using hard times to please God.

3. Matthew 27:45–46 helps bring together the Christological perspective and situational aspect of the psalms. "From the sixth hour until the ninth hour darkness came over the land. About the ninth hour Jesus cried out in a loud voice, *Eloi, Eloi, lama sabachthani?* which means, 'My God, my God why have you forsaken me?'" Especially in the psalms, Jesus is the ideal man realized. In many of the psalms (see above and page 105), the psalmist is often faced with forsakenness. It is real to him—he feels it—but it in actuality, it is a *perceived* forsakenness. How so? Picture the scene at the cross. Darkness and silence fills the land as Jesus faces His Father as Judge

and bears God's wrath. On the cross, before He breathed His last, at the conclusion of God's judgment and the full payment of the penalty of lawbreaking, Jesus cried out to the Father. Think of the irony of that cry. Jesus, the second person of the Trinity and the eternal son of God, knew full well the answer. He knew that God could not forsake God, but that, as the God-man, He must be completely forsaken judicially. It was a fearful and agonizing thing for Jesus to fall into the hands of the living God (Heb. 10:31). Christ had been preparing Himself for this moment. With a new resolve, He had turned His face toward Jerusalem (Luke 9:51). John, in chapter 11 of his gospel, gives a preview of Jesus's forsakenness and His response to it. In Romans 8:35–37, Paul captures this great truth for believers. He reminds believers that they are in Christ and supra-conquerors because Christ was forsaken in their place.

4. Jesus's *true* forsakenness contrasts the *perceived* forsakenness of any and every believer in whatever state, including the psalmist and Job. Since Christ has been forsaken, no believer will ever be forsaken. A person's feelings may tell them differently, but biblical truth and its application is far superior to being led by mere feelings. We must teach this truth to our people. Some have described this anguish as the "dark night of the soul": intense inner-man angst. What is the source of the angst? Dr. Boice, in his commentary on Psalm 88, writes

that it is "a state of intense spiritual anguish in which the struggling, despairing believer *feels* that he is abandoned by God."[17] Dr. Boice does not define spiritual anguish, but he gives an insight into his thinking when he uses the word "feel." In fact, no believer is ever forsaken, because Christ was forsaken in his place. We do know that Jesus was faced with trouble—pressure, from within and from without—all of His life. His preeminent temptation was that of covenantal unfaithfulness—to use His power and authority for personal gain, including relief. Throughout His Messianic ministry, beginning in the wilderness and culminating at the cross, Jesus was faced with the choice of whom He would serve (Matt. 4:1–11; Luke 4:1–13). Jesus proved Himself to be the true Adam and the true Psalmist. These truths are especially applicable to people with psychiatric labels.

5. We know the pressure that Jesus experienced was not from sinful thinking, wanting, and acting (see footnote 14). Jesus, the God-man, was engaged as a whole person and He responded in a God-glorifying manner. John Calvin writes: "In short, during his fearful torture his faith remained uninjured, so that, while he complained of being forsaken, he still

---

17   James M. Boice, *Psalms, Volume 2: Psalms 42–106, An Expositional Commentary* (Ada, MI: Baker, 2005) 716.

relied on the aid of God as at hand."[18] In contrast to Job, Jesus did not live the lie, but held fast to God's promises and was victorious (Heb. 12:1–3; see my book *Endurance: What It is and What It Looks Like in the Believer's Life*).[19] Jesus focused on the situation God's way for God's glory. The dark night is *not* the situation, but the person's response to it. Jesus demonstrated how to handle the most severe aspect of God's providence. Jesus had bad feelings. He was *not* depressed. He used the situation for a great good. So, too, must every believer.

6. The book of Job is quite helpful in this regard as well. Job functioned out of a vital and dynamic relationship with God (Job 1:1–3, 8; 2:2:3). It is in this context that Job perceives God's presence as heaviness (the Hebrew word *kabod*): a burden rather than a blessing (Job 23:2; 33:7). Dissatisfied with his counselors, Job demanded an audience with God and an explanation. However, when God con-

---

18   Calvin's *Commentaries*, Volume XVII, page 319. Calvin's use of the word "complain" seems appropriate. By it he can't mean that Christ was a grumbler. Calvin also wrote on page 319: "still in his heart faith, he remained firm, by which he beheld the presence of God, of whose absence he complains [*grieves over*–JH]." Surely Calvin is speaking of the incomprehensible anguish in Jesus's inner person previewed in John 11. Jesus knew full well Num. 11:1–23, 16:1–50, and 21:1–9.

19   Dr. Jim Halla, *Endurance: What It is and What It Looks Like in the Believer's Life* (Greenville, SC: Ambassador, 2012).

fronted Job about Himself, Job eventually repented (Job 42:6). Only then was he restored spiritually and materially. Others shared in that blessing (Job 42).

A fourth reason for the often unquestioned acceptance by Christians of the rationale behind the medical diagnosis of depression is the Bible's lack of a formal definition of depression. On the other hand, the Bible does describe the spectrum of human experience both from God's perspective *and* the perspective of suffering, sinful individuals. The Bible provides God's way for victory.

A fifth reason why it is easy to accept the medical diagnosis of depression is the presumed *safety* of following traditional medical practice. Most physicians have accepted the Medical Model to explain symptoms even if there is no definite explanatory pathology. Culture and most physicians accept the Greek (and pagan) dualistic, psychosomatic jargon to explain symptoms. However, not entirely satisfied with the Medical Model, some medical personnel accept that man has a spiritual component. Accordingly, they have adopted the Biopsychosocial and/or Biopsychosocial-spiritual model of symptoms.[20] Either way, the Bible is not used, or is used only as adjunctive therapy.

---

20   Biopsychosocial model (BPS) of disease: Due to the failure of the Medical Model of disease at least in some areas, many practitioners have moved toward the BPS in an effort to emphasize the importance of biology (nature), psychological factors (the so-called deep issues of man), and social and environmental factors (nurture). This model divides man into multiple compartments and assigns each of them to an expert. The Biopsychosocial-

When the term *help* (see the earlier comment regarding the term *depression*) is not defined or is defined differently than in the Bible, the Bible will not be used to address the whole person, or it will be used improperly. For instance, acceptance of the secular model and definition of depression, may well lead a person to conclude that individuals such as Paul (2 Cor. 1:8–10; 4:8–10) and even Jesus (when He was in the Garden of Gethsemane and on the cross) *struggled* with depression. Such a conclusion has far-reaching implications.

> We do not want you to be uninformed, brothers and sisters, about the hardships we suffered in the province of Asia. We were under great pressure, far beyond our ability to endure, so that we despaired even of life. Indeed, in our hearts we felt the sentence of death. But this happened that we might not rely on ourselves but on God, who raises the dead. He has delivered us from such a deadly peril, and he will deliver us. On him we have set our hope that he will continue to deliver us.
>
> – 2 Cor. 1:8–10

spiritual (BPSS) model adds a spiritual dimension to man's make-up. This model postulates that spiritual variables are fundamental determinants of psychological, physical, and social factors, which play a role in producing or aggravating a person's condition. In the context of the BPSS, "spiritual" has no relation to the Holy Spirit.

> We are hard pressed on every side, but not
> crushed; perplexed, but not in despair; perse-
> cuted, but not abandoned; struck down, but not
> destroyed; We always carry around in our body
> the death of Jesus so that the life of Jesus may
> also be revealed in our body.
>
> – 2 Cor.4:8–10

In 2 Corinthians 1:8–10; 4:8–10, Paul considered himself without resources to the point of being perplexed
and uncertain whether he would live. In 2 Corinthians
1:8 and 4:8, the word in the original is *exaporeo,* and
it carries with it the idea of being wholly without resources—to be at a loss, humanly-speaking. (The same
word is used in Psalm 88:15 in the Septuagint; see footnote 34). Given his circumstances, Paul thought—he
concluded—that his death was imminent. In chapter 1,
Paul reflects on his experiences. In verse 9, he writes
that God's purpose was to strip him of self-reliance
(see 2 Cor. 12:7–10 for a similar lesson). In verse 10, he
pictures God as the purposeful Deliverer upon Whom
he actively, cognitively, and purposefully set his hope.
In chapter 4, verses 8–10, Paul is drawing attention to
his troubles and his response to them for the benefit of
the Corinthians as well as himself. Today, Paul might
very well have received the diagnosis of depression on
the basis of what he said. Paul had bad feelings, but not
because of unbiblical thinking and desires (also see 2 Cor.

6:3–10; 11:23–29). He did not stop functioning or fail to be responsible. He did not give up or give into his feelings; they were not his guide. Paul was *not* depressed.

Others may use the Bible and the person's relationship with Christ in a supporting, user-friendly role, much like one would use an antidepressant, a Xanax, alcohol, or a cigarette. A vignette concerning one of my patients highlights this. Daily she complained of pain and feeling bad. She awakened at night and prayed to God for relief. When relief did not come, she took a Xanax. I asked her if that was a proper response to God's "no." She said getting relief was the most important thing at that moment. I asked her to think about her relationship to God in Christ and its impact on her thoughts, desires, and actions, and feelings, especially when things weren't going her way. She told me she had no idea she was using God and functioning as if her relationship with Christ was no better, and sometimes less effective, than a Xanax.

Medicine would like us to believe that bad-feeling states are physical in nature, and therefore are fair game for medication. Following this lead, believers say <u>that</u> since depression is a physical problem (that is, something is wrong with the body), medications are to be used as God's gift. One might even say <u>that</u> God gave us medication to help the body. So why shouldn't a believer take any drug <u>that</u> makes them feel better, such as antidepressants? The short answer is this: the goal in life is *not* better feelings. When getting better feelings is the

major emphasis for going to the doctor, or to church,
long-lasting good feelings (defined biblically as contentment) will not come.[21] More importantly, God will not
be honored. Rather, good stewardship for God's glory
is to be the motive for every believer:

> *So we make it our goal to please him, whether we are at*
> *home in the body or away from it.*

> — 2 Cor. 5:9

> *But seek first his kingdom and his righteousness, and all these*
> *things will be given to you as well.*

> — Matt. 6:33

Do Psychological Labels Help or Hinder?

Pragmatically speaking, does the label of "depression"
help anyone? I submit that it actually detracts from and
hinders the use of biblical truth. How, you ask? Let me
preface my answer with a personal experience. Following a report I delivered at a meeting of my church's
presbytery (a group of men who meet to discuss church
life) regarding biblical counseling, I was asked if I had
ever met a good psychiatrist. I failed miserably in my
response, partly because I failed to have the questioner

---

21   See my teaching notes entitled *The Biblical View of Illness and Physical
Problems* and the pamphlet *A Biblical Approach to Receiving Medical Care* at my
website, jimhalla.com. In them, I address such subjects as stewardship of the
whole person and the use and non-use of medications.

define "good psychiatrist." In my failure, I have come to realize that *three* terms need clarity: depression, help/better, and good. I previously addressed the terms *depression* and *help*, and now I will address the term *good*.

Jesus defined *good* in response to the rich young ruler's question regarding inheriting eternal life (Matt. 19:1–2; Mark 10:17–18; Luke 18:18–19). Jesus began with a proper vertical reference: only God is good. Since God is good and He is truth, only biblical truth rightly applied is good and only it sets the person free from his bondage (John 14:6, 17:17; 8:31–32—Jesus and the Word are Truth). The person labeled as having depression is in bondage to himself and his perceived lack of resources and control. So often this mindset is unrecognized, unacknowledged, and even denied. Untruth or *partial truth* is counterfeit, and holds the person in bondage. The person chooses to remain in the dark, blaming his bad feelings for his decision (John 3:16–21, 36; Rom. 1:18–20).

I realize that psychiatry and psychology are not synonymous. I will leave the subject of psychiatry and psychology for another time. Suffice it to say that there are more than 250 theories of psychology. I failed to ask the questioner which psychological theory a "good psychiatrist" would accept, on what basis, and how he justified its use when faced with such passages as 2 Timothy 3:16–17 and 2 Peter 1:3–4.

Help and *better* must be defined according to biblical truth as well. Applied truth moves a person to become more like Christ, as the person functions like a Christian "oyster."[22] Just as an oyster uses a grain of sand to create a beautiful pearl, the believer is to use the unpleasantness of his situations to make the pearl of Christlikeness. 2 Corinthians 5:9 teaches this concept: "So we make it our goal to please Him whether we are at home in the body or away from it." Since the God-ordained way to please God is growth in Christlikeness, true help must be judged on the biblical standard such as given in 2 Corinthians 5:9.

Going back to the presbytery meeting, I would ask my questioner: "Does psychiatry, as a discipline rooted in non-biblical dogma, help a person become more like Christ? If so, how?" The answers, by necessity, are no. Only biblical truth rightly applied by and to a changed heart, illumined by the Holy Spirit, motivates the believer to become more like Christ (Phil. 2:12–13; 2 Pet. 3:18). The believer grows because God has worked in him and the believer is responding to God's work. The believer's growth is testimony of God's inward work.

The use of various psychological labels hinders the use of biblical truth for a number of reasons. One is the cultural mindset that relief is the major therapeutic goal for bad feelings. This mantra permeates homes, coffee

---

22   An oyster has been created with the capacity to take an irritant—sand— and fashion it into something beautiful—a pearl. The believer is to function in a similar fashion: using unpleasantness to develop the character of Christ. This is one lesson of the cross.

shops, counseling rooms, and doctor's offices. *Self* thus takes center stage. People are considered victims of their feelings and their environment. Consequently people, physicians, and counselors often deny or ignore the fact that their situation is from God's good, purposeful, and providential hand. When that happens, people are encouraged to grumble and complain against God.

All people live out of an identity (see footnotes 7, 8, 12). This is God's creational design. Often, though, people take on the identity of the label that they have been given, thinking, "I am that label." For instance, Adam was created a dependent creature. God entered into a covenant (agreement) with him. God identified Adam as a covenant-keeper. He was called to covenantal faithfulness. As such, he was to serve and glorify God with all his heart. Initially, Adam accepted his position and he enjoyed fellowship with God and His presence was not a burden. Because Adam represented all mankind, God has identified every person as a theologian and covenant keeper.

Post–Fall, Adam and every person became a covenant breaker and a *mis-labeler*. Often a person accepts a label from others in a way that was not part of God's original plan. The label often motivates the one receiving the label to ignore, reject, and replace the label that God has given to every person: "a dependent creature with a vertical relationship." Labels serve many functions:

- as motivation for a person's thoughts and desires.

> Feelings and actions follow;

- as an explanation for thoughts, desires, and action (or inaction);
- as a refuge and source of comfort;
- as an agenda-setter for the pursuit of some goal.

In bad-feeling states, relief is not only the goal but also the *reason* for the person's thinking, wanting, and doing. People who report bad feelings often are inactive. On the other hand, the believer has a new label, by virtue of membership in a new kingdom and family with a new Father, union with Christ, and the indwelling Holy Spirit. The believer's heart is changed so they can think God's thoughts, desire what God desires, and act obediently. Their functional belief system and functional motivational center have been radically changed at regeneration. As a result, the believer is not constrained to act out of some label given to them by the secular community. In fact, they are motivated to function as a child of the King and a supra-conqueror (see Rom. 8:35–39). Ministering biblical truth to the whole person is key in any situation, especially with those people labeled as having bad-feeling states.[23]

---

23   Martin Lloyd-Jones, discussing reasons for studying the subject he calls "spiritual depression," says it this way. First, he writes that looking at the Bible first is always "a good way of facing any problem." He gives a second reason on page 11: "In a sense a depressed Christian is a contradiction in terms, and is a very poor recommendation for the gospel." On page 23 he writes: "The first

To counter the resource-less, relief-is-everything mindset, I ask my patients and counselees how it is possible that something outside of them *makes* them feel the way they do. Most are clueless how to answer. Since they come to me with their complaints of bad feelings, expressed in a variety of ways, I meet them at the feeling level. But as I gather data by asking questions, I move to their thoughts and desires/wants. Nothing and no one touched them physically, yet they feel bad. The very presence of another person or a situation seems to have *caused* their bad feelings. They are faced with a dilemma: cause versus trigger. By this time, they begin to consider that their responses are driven by thoughts and desires and often demands. I move them to accept God's creational design that thoughts and desires are the result of both inner- and outer-man activities. I have them reflect on the situation as the *context* and not the *cause* of their feelings. I have them connect their thoughts and desires with their feelings *and* their response. Most people are willing to consider that they are not victims to that which is outside of them. Some people appreciate this insight, while others are threatened by it. Many people have trained themselves to *react* from a victim and label mentality. A reactive mode requires

is that it is sad that anybody should remain in such a condition. But the second reason is still more serious and important, that is that such people are very poor representatives of the Christian faith." Martin Lloyd-Jones, *Spiritual Depression: Its Causes and Its Cure* (Grand Rapids, MI: Eerdmans, 1965) 10–11, 23.

less effort and less discipline. It is easier to react than to *respond* from a biblically-controlled mindset.

A second reason that the use of various psychological labels hinders the use of biblical truth is the liberalization of the definition of *depression* by the secular community (see footnote 14). As a consequence, the frequency of finding "depressed" people in our society is high. According to current medical dogma, some type of treatment is therefore mandatory.

A third reason centers on what is being taught about depression. Even for a believer, depression seems to be an expected and normal response to life. I reiterate: the terms *life* and *theologian* are often misused and misunderstood, even by Christians who think that life "just is" and can be lived with an improper reference to God and without consequences. Rather, a person's situation is the result of God's providence—His good, purposeful, and orderly control. This is an important fact. Words do matter. Following the secular mindset and taken to its logical conclusion, God would be considered responsible for bad feelings. Such a conclusion leads to further trust in self, and thus further hopelessness and further misery. In essence, depressed people are considered victims to their *nature* and *nurture;* yet both of these are under God's sovereign control. In the final analysis, the person functions as if he has been victimized by God.[24]

---

24   It may be that a depression-causing (or a bad-feeling-causing) gene will be discovered (or any other gene that makes it easy for a person to react with

A fourth reason is the tendency to follow the Medical Model. Based on the Medical Model, depression is considered a *physical* problem. However, a physical examination and laboratory testing are not needed for a diagnosis of depression. Even though depression is characterized by feelings and feeling-directed behavior, the diagnosis of depression leads to the conclusion, especially by the person, that something is wrong *with* (not only *in*) the body. The medical community would probably deny that behavior is driven by feelings. However, I reiterate, the Bible teaches that man lives out of his heart. Behavior is driven by feelings, which are influenced by thoughts and desires. While behavior is observable and not subjective, it is observer-dependent and interpreted according to a standard. In other words, when one considers any psychological condition, subjectivity rules. Bad feelings, verbalized in some form, are thus the major criteria for

---

fear, worry, or anger). Does that mean that my body and God made me do it? Is "ease of feeling down" the answer to poor functioning? It is possible that some people may become depressed (or worried, fearful, anxious, or obese) more easily than others. The ease could be physical: genes, for instance. If that is the case, the believer, aware of the fact, should diligently practice biblically-controlled thinking and wanting *before* faced with situational triggers. Biblically-controlled thinking and wanting are to become a radically different way of life—a new habituation—for the believer. In that way triggers won't be feared, but embraced and used as a tool to become more like Christ. Functioning as a Christian oyster (footnote 22) is always possible and proper, no matter a person's genes or situation. Both come from God's hand.

the diagnosis of depression. Biblically, a person's behavior is influenced by how he feels. How he feels is controlled and motivated by his thoughts and desires. The link between thinking, wanting (desires), actions, and feelings is biblically correct and undeniable.

Contrast the "Subjectivity Rules" Approach with gathering data in a biblical manner (see footnote 10). With this approach, feelings reign supreme and are the criteria for diagnosis and the success or failure of treatment. Biblical data gathering is accomplished by asking questions from the inside out regarding thoughts, desires, and actions. You inquire about the person's motivation. God has made us inside-out people (Prov. 4:23: "Above else, guard your heart; for it is the wellspring of life"; Matt. 12:33–36, 15:7–9, 16–20; Mark 7:6–8, 18–23). Attitudes and beliefs originate in the heart and become ingrained in the whole person. A patterned lifestyle of thinking and wanting is established. The body, including the brain, becomes habituated so that a person reacts as if thinking and wanting play no role in his response. Thoughts and desires give rise to actions and feelings, which are mostly, but not exclusively, outer-man activities (see also footnotes 5, 7, 8, 10, 12, 25).

Ponder the above truths. They should not be divorced from the believer's prior membership in Satan's family and kingdom. Every person was in Adam by God's design. Adam was designated by God to be the head of the human race. What Adam did, God counted every person, born by ordinary generation, to have done. As a result of Adam's first sin and God's judgment, all mankind was lost and every person became a member of Satan's family and kingdom. Thus, everyone at some point was unsaved. Every person thought, desired, and acted like Satan. In John 8:44, Jesus said: "You belong to your father, the devil, and you want to carry out your father's desire. He was a murderer from the beginning, not holding to the truth, for there is no truth in him." This statement applies to every unbeliever, but the believer can and does function as if he is unsaved.

Jesus's words to Peter in Matthew 16:23 clarify this point: "Get behind me Satan! You are a stumbling block to me; you do not have in mind the things of God, but the things of men." Membership in Satan's family and kingdom has severe consequences, one of which is summarized by the frequently misunderstood doctrine of total depravity (Gen. 6:5–6; 8:21; Ps. 51:1–4; 14:1; 53:1; Rom. 3:9–19; 8:5–8; Eph. 2:1–3). No part of man was untouched by sin. His nature and his whole-person activity—thoughts, desires, and actions—became anti-God and pro-self. In a real sense, every person has been under Satan's tutelage; they have become habituated to his ways of thinking, wanting, and getting (Matt. 13:38; Acts 13:10; Eph. 2:2; 1 John 3:8–10).

The Bible pictures this habituation in several ways. One is man's animal-like activities of *getting*. Esau is a perfect example of sensual orientation as contrasted to suprasensual living (see footnotes 7, 8, 10, 12, 25, 31–32, 35–37). In Genesis 25:29–34, Moses wrote that Esau was guided by his stomach—his senses—unchecked by biblical truth. Paul captures this biblical truth in Philippians 3:19: "Their destiny is destruction, their god is their stomach, and their glory is their shame. Their mind is on earthly things." Consumed by a "have it now" theology of life, Esau sold his birthright for the good feeling that food supplied (also see Psalm 73, especially verses 16–22). James addresses this issue in James 3:15: "Such wisdom does not come down from heaven but is earthly, unspiritual, of the devil." James warns against the "wisdom from below." The word that James and the Holy Spirit chose in the original that is translated "from the devil" is *psuchikos* (1 Cor. 2:14; 15:44, 46; Jude 19; Prov. 12:1, 30:2). The word draws a contrast between earthly, man-derived, and self-centered "wisdom" (which is not wisdom at all!) and true wisdom, which is Holy Spirit-given and directed.

The idea conveyed by *psuchikos* is "the natural, animal-like activity of getting." As a result of man's corrupt nature and prior membership in Satan's kingdom, man is *instinctively* a getter, self-oriented, anti-God, and a user of others. The picture is not a pretty one. But thanks be to God that believers have been rescued from Satan and his kingdom as well as from self, from the world, and from God and His judgment (Rom. 7:25; 8:1; Col. 1:13; Gal. 1:3–4; 2 Pet. 1:3–4; 1 John 2:15–17). The believer can and does think God's thoughts and desire God's desires, enabling him to act as a God pleaser. The believer's battle can be summarized by the biblical dynamic of "putting off" and "putting on" (Eph. 4:22–24; Col. 3:8–10; Rom. 13:12–14). Daily, and moment by moment, the believer (and only he can do this) must, and will, put off ingrained habits of thinking, wanting, and doing that were practiced and learned so well while under Satan's influence. He must—and he will—replace his old habits by putting on new habits of thinking, wanting, and doing. He must, and will, move from sensual living to suprasensual living. He must, and will, put off himself and self-pleasing and put on Christ and God-pleasing. Praise God!

When I spend time with patients and counselees who have been diagnosed with depression, what stands out is the relation between feeling *and* thinking, wanting, and doing. Proper data gathering, as previously described, should lead to the inevitable conclusion that people labeled with depression are like everyone else, in that they are thinkers and wanters—not simply feelers. Verbs denote action; this is part of the reason the term *depressed* is misleading. Depression is usually viewed as something happening to someone or in someone. People in bad-feeling states are reactors. The person considers himself acted upon. In that sense, depression is passive. However, biblically speaking, the whole person is active in any feeling state. Based on the person's previous and current thoughts and desires, he makes certain conclusions about himself, God, others, and situations. I reiterate: a person's interpretive grid is either God's word or it is the triad that I have mentioned several times: the person's feelings, his reason divorced or wrongly associated with biblical truth, and/or his experience.

When faced with unpleasantness, people whose authority and guide are their feelings find it easy to functionally and actively give up on God, His promises, and the application of biblical principles to their situation. As a consequence, and in varying degrees, they neglect some or many of their God-designed responsibilities. Such a person cognitively and willfully gives up, even though he or she may deny that fact, or explain it away by bad feelings and then asserting their right to do so. Many, if not most, people labeled as being depressed have trained themselves to rely on feelings. Feeling or sensual living is part of the legacy of membership in Satan's kingdom and family.[25] In many instances, those

---

25   In marked contrast to sensual living (footnotes 7–8, 10, 12, 25, 35, 37), the Bible calls for suprasensual living (2 Cor. 5:7). By that term I mean biblically-controlled thinking and wanting patterned after Christ (John 4:31–34). Suprasensual living, too, is faith-based: saving faith. Its basis is the believer's salvation and what he is in Christ. He is new creature (2 Cor. 5:17), indwelt with the Holy Spirit. He has the mind of Christ, which is the Holy Spirit (contrast 1 Cor. 2:14 and 2:16). The unbeliever has eyes and ears but he does not see or hear because there is no inner-man change: his heart is far away from God (Isa. 6:9–10; Matt. 13:13–15). The believer has had his eyes opened and he sees (Mark 7:34). He interprets information through the eyes of saving faith. What he takes in by his senses he filters by

carrying the label of depression have developed *learned hopelessness* and *helplessness*. I would agree that such a person has taken action, but that action has been to give in to feelings while ignoring biblical truth. That person's proper reference to God and to others have been replaced by an inordinate self-focus.

I often hear the refrain that depression (a noun) "just is" and "I can't help myself." Depression is often presented as an uncontrollable bad feeling of "I just feel down and out, so I don't do anything." However, the verb confirms what some people say: "I can depress myself any time I want, about anything."[26] Conversely, people can un-depress themselves as well. Psalms 42 and 43 give helpful insight into this matter. Three times in these chapters, the psalmist asks himself why he is downcast and disturbed within: in 42:5, 42:11, and 43:5. The Hebrew word for *downcast* is in the active voice and refers to a "pressing or casting down." The psalmist asks

---

a completely different interpretive instrument—a changed inner-man. As a result, the believer has a different perspective and orientation for life. He has a different goal (John 4:31–34; 2 Cor. 5:9) and a different motivation. He lives *not* for self but for God, Who is his Lord (2 Cor. 5:14–15). The believer works out his salvation by becoming more like Christ (Phil. 2:12–13; Rom. 8:28–29; 2 Cor. 3:18). He is not under the circumstances, but he is a victor in Christ (Rom. 8:35–39).

26   Several secular counseling systems, including William Glasser (*Reality Therapy* and *Choice Theory*), agree that a person depresses himself by wrong thinking. In my own practice and counseling ministry, person after person confirms this fact in some form or another.

himself why is he casting himself down and inflicting misery on himself; why is he depressing himself?

His inner-man angst (the word for "disturbed within" describes agitation, and being stirred up) was connected with his view of himself, his circumstances, and the God of his circumstances. He recognized that the circumstances did not cause him to think and desire the way he did; rather, the circumstances exposed his true self. The psalmist understood the seriousness of his wrong thinking. He counseled himself to hope in the Lord, implying that his hope had been self-focused and in something else. He acknowledged the reality of hard times, *but* he also acknowledged the God *of them* and *of him*. His God had not forsaken him. The psalmist came to his senses and responded correctly (see Luke 15:17–20).

A similar experience is recorded in Psalm 73:21–26 (especially verse 22), Asaph, the author of Psalm 73, describes his initial response to the prosperity of the wicked as a self-centered "woe is me," "me first," and "look at what am I missing." The psalmist's acknowledgement and acceptance of God's presence and an eternal perspective of life moved him to rely on God instead of on himself.[27]

---

27 Martin Lloyd-Jones addresses the issue of depressing oneself. He concludes that at the root of "spiritual depression" is unbelief, and he recommends knowing yourself and knowing biblical truth. Also see chapters 1 and 2, pages 35–43, in volume 1 of John Calvin's *Institutes of the Christian Religion*, edited by

The psalmist of Psalms 42 and 43 *stilled* himself before God. He acknowledged that, functionally, he was attempting to push God off His throne. The psalmist ceased striving, because he realized that fundamentally he was competing with (striving against) God. He acknowledged that God was God and that he wasn't (see Psalm 46:10). He focused on the Lord and His promises and followed the path described in Psalm 131:2: "but I have stilled and quieted my soul; like a weaned child with its mother, like a weaned child is my soul within me." He encouraged himself by these facts. He changed his thoughts and desires about God, His presence and control, about himself, and about his circumstances. His

---

J.T. McNeil (Philadelphia: Westminster, 1960). Calvin contends that knowledge of God leads to knowledge of self and vice versa. The truth will set you free (John 8:31–32). The best definition for Dr. Jones' term "spiritual depression" is in his foreword. There he describes soul-strugglers (my term) as unhappy people struggling with their problems. On page 54, he urges his readers to "read the words and you can almost see the man looking cast down and dejected. You can almost see it in his face." On page 54, he equates depression and unhappiness. Dr. Jones seems to focus on feelings, suffering, and behavior—not unlike the psychological approach and label. And yet his solution is the faithful application of biblical truth to what he calls mind, heart, and will. In chapter five he refers to the whole person, but does not truly emphasize man as a whole person or duplex being. However, in essence, Dr. Jones champions the necessity of ministering to the whole person, knowing that thoughts, desires, and actions are linked. I say "amen." Martin Lloyd-Jones, *Spiritual Depression: Its Causes and its Cure* (Grand Rapids, MI: Eerdmans, 1988) 13–19, 54.

own control and presumed lack of resources were no longer issues. Praising God, he set his hope on God rather than on himself and the relief he wanted (2 Cor. 1:8–10; 4:8–10 as discussed on pages 59–60). The psalmist got busy doing something, but the specifics of his actions are not described. Make no mistake: thinking, wanting, and doing are interrelated, and feelings are linked to them. God doesn't separate them and neither must we.

Some patients and counselees deny their self-depressing capacity, saying they don't know why they are depressed, rather they only *feel*. These facts alone should lead you to the biblical conclusion that thinking, wanting, doing (or not doing), and feeling are linked. Even the secular community utilizes God's creational design of man as a duplex being and whole person. Yet they deny God and His work when they recommend psychotherapy or cognitive behavioral therapy as treatment for depression. Changed thoughts and desires can and do ameliorate symptoms, even when divorced from our Sovereign Creator God.

An interaction with a patient and counselee highlights many of the points discussed above. An older widow, who is a life-long believer, told me that she had had a hard life. Her story covered twenty-five years of being sinned against, sinning in return, broken relationships, loss of loved ones, estranged family, and physical problems. Pain and inability to function were ever-present realities. She had gone to her family physician and received antidepressants. She still cried and felt bad. She told me that her "mountain looked so high" and her "hole looked so deep." I asked her where God fit into her thinking and wanting. She said that if it had not been for God she would not have made it through. She said the presence of God made it easy for her to pray. She was convinced that God was with her.

I asked her to reconcile her crying and her complaint of bad feelings with her belief in an ever-present God. She said she couldn't. She knew God was there and His there-ness enabled her to pray, but she was still depressed. Initially, she did not see the disconnect. She said she could not explain her feelings. I asked her to tell me her thinking and wanting when she was depressed. She told me that she focused on what she did not want but had (a broken body, no husband, and the past sins against her and her sinful responses) and what she wanted and did not have (relief and a changed life). She was able to confess her self focus. That realization was a new concept for her. She said she felt worse "all over" when she focused on herself and the unpleasantness of her life. Next I asked about her focus, thoughts, and desires when she prayed. Without hesitation, she told me that she had an entirely different focus—on God and His presence.

She came to realize that she was depressing herself. She understood that right thinking and right wanting might not change her body's problems and bad feelings, but it enabled her to be satisfied and contented. She came to appreciate the beauty of pleasing God, which has its own reward. Now when she begins to feel blue and depress herself, she focuses on good stewardship of her whole person. As a child of the King, the God who is there is truly there, and that fact is satisfying in its own right.

A non-jaundiced look at psychological labels and people so labeled shows that the emphasis on helping people should be on changing their thoughts and desires from the inside out, rather than changing their feelings and behavior. Again, the connection between thinking, wanting, and doing as whole-person activities must be addressed. Biblical truth is God's tool for addressing the whole person and it should be ours.

To date, psychological labels have not been scientifically proven to be based on abnormal genes, molecules, or neurotransmitters. Psychiatry would like us to believe that some or all these factors play a role in depression. To the chagrin of many psychiatrists, colleagues and scientists in other fields agree that there is still much debate about whether psychiatry is indeed a science.[28]

---

28   Bruce E Levine, "Psychiatry Now Admits It's Been Wrong in Big Ways---But Can It Change?", Truthout website, dated March 5, 2014, accessed April 1, 2014, http://www.truth-out.org/news/item/22266-psychiatry-now-admits-its-been-wrong-in-big-ways-but-can-it-change.

Philip Hickey, PhD, "Psychiatry Is Not Based On Valid Science," on the website Mad In America: Science, Psychiatry and Community, dated January 9, 2014, accessed April 1, 2014, http://www.madinamerica.com/2014/01/psychiatry-based-valid-science/.

"How a Scientific Field Can Collapse: The Case of Psychiatry," on the website Evolution News & Views, dated May 8, 2013, accessed April 1, 2014, http://www.evolutionnews.org/2013/05/how_a_scientifi071931.html.

On the other hand, if psychiatry did prove itself a science and did prove that depression is a physical problem, where would that leave pastors, biblical counselors, and Christian physicians? I think it would leave us right where we are. How, you say? Medicine has been able to classify a number of physical problems as diseases, such as diabetes, rheumatoid arthritis, cancer, and neurological-brain diseases such as Alzheimer's. These conditions are associated with pathology in the material part of man, including his brain. The abnormalities are responsible for much, perhaps all, of the person's symptoms and signs. Christians are urged to pray for people with physical conditions and show them compassion. Doctors may give them biblical material to read. But is there more to be done? Yes, and amen.

One of my goals as a rheumatologist is to help patients function as God's kind of patient. How do I do that? [29] I address the whole person in varying degrees during their office visit and via my handouts covering such subjects as arthritis and rheumatism, pain and one's

Also see footnotes 31, 33 and my teaching notes on the website, jimhalla.com, and in my two books: *Being Christian in Your Medical Practice* and *True Competence in Medicine.*

29   I spell out multiple examples of how-tos, both for patients and physicians alike in my books, *Being Christian in Your Medical Practice* and *Practicing Biblical-Based Medicine in a Fallen World*, and in pamphlets, *What to Do You When Your Body Fails You* and *A Biblical Approach to Receiving Medical Care.* These and other materials are available without charge on my website: jimhalla.com.

response to it, stress, and pain relief. I remind patients of several factors: all bodies are failing, some more rapidly than others; biblical principles address fully this aspect of life; taking care of their body is a God-given blessing as a well as a privilege and requirement.

Good stewardship is beneficial in its own right. Truly God's truth, rightly applied, sets people free (John 8:31-32). Nothing is hidden or out of bounds for God's people in His Word. Therefore, even if a physical cause were to be proven for depression (it hasn't been), biblical principles are still required to be *taught* by the pastor, physician, and counselor and used by the person. Biblically-controlled thinking and wanting, not medication, help guard against feeling-oriented living (which is often the source of bad feelings) and help replace unbiblical thinking and wanting for those who have given in to feelings (the response to bad feelings). Moreover, because of the duplex nature of man, right thinking and wanting have a healthy effect on the person no matter his physical problem (see Prov. 3:5–8; 12:25; 14:30; 15:13, 30; 16:24; 17:30).

Helping a person come to the realization that there is a far superior goal in life than merely relief from bad feelings is a monumental theological endeavor. Pleasing God is what every believer was designed for in eternity past and regenerated to do at some point in time (Eph. 1:4; John 3:3–8; Titus 3:5). Pleasing God by becoming more like Christ brings satisfaction and contentment in this life, and, in part, is a foretaste of heaven (Rom. 8:28–29;

2 Cor. 3:18; Matt. 11:28–30). These truths are especially important for those who carry psychiatric labels.

God has not stopped a person's ministry and growth in Christlikeness because of his failing body or bad-feeling state. Rather, God has changed the person's context and perhaps the direction of his ministry. Failing bodies are to be used as the oyster uses the sand to make a pearl (2 Cor. 5:9). You might say, "Whoa, Halla! The person can't do that. He feels so bad, plus he has a body problem—therefore he is depressed." My question to you is this: If the body is the sole problem, what are we to do with the Bible's teaching regarding the whole-person activities of thoughts, desires, and actions? Consider these biblical truths as you answer:

Thoughts:

For who has known the mind of the Lord that he may instruct him? But we have the mind of Christ.

– 1 Cor. 2:16

We demolish arguments and every pretension that sets itself up against the knowledge of God and we take captive every thought to make it obedient to Christ.

– 2 Cor. 10:5

Finally brothers whatever is true, whatever is noble, whatever is right, whatever is pure, whatever is lovely,

> *whatever is admirable—if anything is excellent or praiseworthy—think about such things.*
>
> — Phil. 4:8

Desires:

> *I desire to do your will, O my God; your law is written within my heart.*
>
> — Ps. 40:8

> *Surely you desire truth in the inner parts; you teach me wisdom in the utmost place.*
>
> — Ps. 51:6

Actions:

> *If you love me, you will obey what I command.*
>
> — John 14:15

> *This is love for God: to obey his commands. And his commands are not burdensome.*
>
> — 1 John 5:3

When the brain is failing, there will be a limited capacity for the use of biblical truth. However, it is a major leap to say that people diagnosed with bad-feeling states *can't* think, desire, and act according to biblical truth (see 1 Cor. 10:13 and Jay Adams's booklet, *Christ and Your Problems*).[30] Hope

---

30   Jay E. Adams, *Christ and Your Problems* (P & R Publishing, 1992).

is a key message of this passage. Too often, "I can't" means "I won't." Saying "I can't" when it refers to pleasing God is tantamount to calling God a liar. The phrase "I can't" must be removed from the believer's vocabulary and replaced by biblical truth such as given in Philippians 4:13: "I can do everything through Him who gives me strength." The "everything" is pleasing God by becoming more like Christ using the unpleasantness of life as God's tool.

Everyone needs to determine how much biblical truth they believe is *not* applicable for people with bad-feeling states, and which part of the Bible they think can and should be eliminated when ministering to them. I have seen it written and heard it said that, "you cannot counsel someone who is not there." "Don't give them any homework." The claim is that people who are depressed can't read or think. The Bible gives an entirely different message. The whole person is there. He may be drowning in his feelings or, more accurately, "feel" as if he is drowning in them. In truth, the problem is in his thinking and wanting. Please note: I am not so much referring to methodology; I am speaking of basic ministry principles. I have given examples of how I apply these principles in this and other of my books.

In regard to bad-feeling states, God has Christians right where He wants us. As true *psychologists* we must imitate Jesus Christ and follow biblical principles. The Greek term *psuche* is used some 104 times in the New Testament. At times it refers to the inner man only and at other times to the whole person. True psychology is the study of the whole person, God's way, for His glory using His self-revelation: the Bible. We must follow Isaiah's proclamation: to the law and testimony (Isa. 8:20). In doing so, we turn to the Bible and glean its truth, especially before we begin with the secular culture's definitions and its "me first" and victimization approach. All facts are to be interpreted through the lens of Scripture, including those discovered by the social and physical sciences. They must be evaluated and interpreted through the grid of biblical truth. Nothing less will truly serve our God and benefit His people.

If you don't agree that thoughts, desires, actions, and feelings are fundamentally involved in bad-feeling states, please follow this suggestion. From the last ten people you have encountered who were labeled with depression, go back and gather data from them to determine their thinking, wanting, doing, and feeling. In some way, each person will relate to you that feelings are their authority and that feelings are linked to their thinking and wanting. Moreover, their thinking and wanting will be out of sync with biblical truth. Feeling-directed behavior always follows. Once you have determined that this is the case, you are in a position to bring biblical truth, rightly applied, to the person where they are, irrespective of any label that has been applied to them. Try it!

Putting It Together

There is a poorly understood link between the inner and outer man; this link is not anatomic. As mentioned previously, what occurs in the inner man *influences* (not causes) activity in the outer man and vice versa. The inner man/outer man connection is pictured in Romans 6:6: "For we know that our old self was crucified with Him so that the body of sin might be done away with that we should no longer be slaves to sin." Among other truths, Romans 6 (also see Rom. 7:14–25) teaches that because of previous membership in Satan's family and kingdom, believers continue to demonstrate, in varying degrees, rebellious self-pleasing. Some theologians attribute man's rebellion to indwelling sin.[31] The West-

---

31   John Owen, "The nature, power, deceit, and prevalency of the remainders of Indwelling Sin," chaps. 1–17 in *The Complete Works of John Owen* (Edinburgh: Banner of Truth, 1966). The question of why believers sin is a subject for another time. Briefly, the Bible teaches that the believer has one nature. Yet he still sins. One explanation is the remaining corruption in the whole person.

minster Confession of Faith speaks of man's remaining corruption (VI:5; IV:4; XIII:2–3; XVII:3). The activity of self-pleasing involves the whole person: thoughts, desires, and actions. These activities occur in both the inner-man and the outer man. At times, self-pleasing may be manifested only in the inner man (Matt. 5:21–22, 28–29; pages 23–24).

In Romans 6, Paul expresses salvation as being crucified with Christ. At salvation, the believer has been radically transferred out of Satan's family and kingdom into God's family and kingdom (see Col. 1:13). As a result of regeneration, the believer has a new nature with the capacity for a new and patterned lifestyle of God-pleasing and God-honoring thinking, wanting, and doing. Paul speaks of this whole-person renewal in 2 Corinthians 5:17: "Therefore, if anyone is in Christ, he is a new cre-

---

What is corruption (depravity)? If we say sin, we have a potential problem. I understand sin to be an anti-God whole-person activity. What is sin? The answer given in the Westminster Shorter Catechism #14 is succinct: Sin is any want [*lack*–JH] of conformity unto, or transgression of, the law of God. That definition emphasizes the ethical and moral quality of sin. I understand sin to be an anti-God, whole-person activity involving thoughts, desires, and actions. In Rom 7:14–15, Paul speaks of sin as an operative principle or law that is present in man—his whole person. Man's nature (*phusis*: refers to an inclination, bent, and orientation), as part of the consequence of the Fall and God's judgment on Adam's first sin, is turned away from God and toward self and Satan. At regeneration man's nature is changed. Please refer to the discussion of this subject throughout the book.

ation, the old has gone, the new has come." The believer has a radically new orientation, bent, and inclination (i.e. a new nature). He has been changed *by* God *for* God. He is recreated to please God rather than self. This fulfils, in time and space, God's eternal decree made in eternity past, as stated in Ephesians 1:4: "For he chose us in him before the creation of the world to be holy and blessed in his sight." As the believer grows in the character of Christ (and he will), his outer-man will be rehabituated as well. Outer-man changes reflect a changed inner man. As a whole person, the believer will be moving toward a proper synchrony within his whole person and between his inner and outer man (see Rom. 8:28–29).

We rejoice with Paul that the believer is no longer a slave to sin (and Satan, self, and the world's ways). In fact, Paul commands a different form of slavery and worship activity in Romans 6:11–20 and 12:1–2. The believer is to present his *whole person* to the Lord. In doing so, he is to be ever mindful of the pull and power of remaining habit patterns of self-pleasing thoughts, desires, and actions that war against a Holy-Spirit-established and -directed mindset and lifestyle. Truly, there is a battle within. The believer does not have two natures. He is a whole person previously under the lordship of Satan and self, but now under the Lordship of Christ. Yet the pull to please self is still strong. However, because of the radical and supernatural change in the inner man, a renewal and rehabituation of both the inner and outer man occurs. The whole-person activity of God-pleasing is termed progressive *sanctification*.[32] In progressive sanctification, the believer closes the gap between what he is in justification (a new record and standing), in adoption (a new status and inheritance), and in positional holiness (a new position), and how he functions. He is a justified and saved sinner, but a sinner nonetheless. Again, biblical truth surfaces: the believer is a whole person, a duplex being, and the image of God such that thinking and wanting influence feeling and doing and vice versa.

Dr. Jay Adams considered the Greek term *sarx* (often translated in the New Testament as "sinful nature") as the sin-habituated body. In part, he based his teaching on passages such as Rom. 6:6; Rom. 7:14–15; James 4:1; 1 Pet. 4:1–2; Matt. 18:8–9; and Mark 9:43, 45, 47. Rightly, I think, he was emphasizing sin's effect on the body in terms of habit formation. I think his emphasis is correct (I discuss this topic later in the book). However, I would not limit habituation to the body but include the whole person: both the inner and outer man.

---

32   A succinct description of sanctification is found in the answer to question 35 of the Westminster Shorter Catechism: "Sanctification is the work of God's free grace whereby the believer is renewed in the whole man after the image of God and is enabled more and more to die unto sin and live unto righteousness." Not arrogantly but for clarity, I think it is helpful to emphasize that the believer also dies to self and Satan's influence that is within the believer as well as outside of him.

As previously noted, man thinks in his brain (in the cerebral cortex and frontal lobe) *and* in his inner man. There is no specific term for brain in the original languages; the brain is part of the body: the *soma*. Culture's view of man's anatomy is incorrect. Biblically, and in contrast to our culture's view, both thinking and wanting are inner- and outer-man activities. The brain receives, interprets, and acts on messages received from various parts of the body. The brain does not stand alone. As such, it is more than a conduit for the expression of inner-man activity. Like the rest of the body, it has become habituated to self-pleasing (see James 4:1: "What causes fights and quarrels among you? Don't they come from your desires that battle within?"). In the original language, "battle within you" is literally "in your members," meaning the physical body and its parts.

In the believer, the inner-man is the place where the Holy Spirit dwells and is active. Inner-man renewal enables the believer to interpret sensory stimuli (that which he takes in by his senses) differently. The Holy Spirit, through His Word, enables the believer to think God's thoughts and desire God's desires. He has the mind of Christ (1 Cor. 2:16). The believer has "eyes to see and ears to hear." As a result of the Holy Spirit's activity, the believer is able to respond in *any* situation according to biblical truth. He can please God because of his whole-person change (see Phil. 2:12–13; 4:13). I repeat: the reason why the believer doesn't consistently function as a God pleaser is the remaining corruption with its habituation and his inclination to please and worship himself. These are an aftermath and legacy of previous membership in Satan's family and kingdom. The remaining corruption results in a spiritual battle—a war—within the believer, as highlighted in such passages as Rom. 7:14–25 and Gal. 5:16–18. The believer is regularly faced with the choice to please God or self.

Unfortunately, our culture and the social sciences (including anthropology, psychology, and sociology) still hold to the pagan lie that feelings are the problem in general and in depression particularly, and therefore these feelings must be changed. As a result, Western medicine is enamored with the following ideas and claims:

- The brain is man's moral compass. In other words, morality is hormones and chemicals and has nothing to do with God's creational design of man as a duplex being and God's image bearer. In contrast to the secular model, the Bible teaches that man is a religious, worshipping, and moral being. As such, his moral compass is located in the heart/inner man and not in the brain.

- Following the Medical Model of disease, that the brain is not functioning correctly due to *nature,* such as genetics, medical science concludes the problem is physical—*with* the body.

- Following the Biopsychosocial and Biopsychosocial-spiritual Models, that the brain is not working correctly due to *nurture* and environmental factors, medical science concludes that the problem is physical, but with a spiritual aspect. The term "spiritual" is unrelated to the Holy Spirit.

- Various chemicals (neurotransmitters) are reported to be awry in patients diagnosed as having depression. Yet several questions are unanswered: What is a normal neurotransmitter level? What is an abnormal neurotransmitter level? If an abnormal level could be proved, is it cause or effect? If there is an imbalance, what is it? What is the role of diurnal variation: do neurotransmitter levels ebb and flow? Does the self-report of feeling better correlate with changed or improved levels? If there is an imbalance, is it correctible on its own, by *faith* of any kind toward any object, cognitive behavioral therapy, medication, or biblically-controlled thinking and wanting?

- Various areas of the brain apparently show different levels of metabolic activity on high tech magnetic resonance imaging (MRI) and positive emission technical (PET) scans. What is the real significance of these changes? Is there a cause and effect relationship? If present, do these change following cognitive behavioral therapy, faith directed in any object, or medications?

- Purported changes in chemical levels of various transmitters and brain blood flow are *causative* for bad feelings, however defined. Is that really true? Are the authors including all bad feelings from whatever source?

- Various inflammatory mediators are abnormally high in those diagnosed with depression and that the inflammatory state *may cause* changes in the nervous system, which in turn *may* cause bad feelings.

- Following the Medical Model of disease, medications are a mainstay of treatment for depression, as well as any number of so-called mental health diseases. However, within the medical community, varying opinions abound on the validity and effectiveness of anti-depressants (footnotes 28, 33).

- Following the Biopsychosocial and Biopsychosocial-spiritual Models of disease, patients are to get in touch with their inner self. There is a focus on removing that which is outside of the person, because "it" is doing something "bad" to the person.

The use of medication and the use of neuroimaging in the diagnosis of depression has been the subject of debate among physicians.[33] And as noted

---

33   Caroline Cassels, "Physicians Go Head to Head in Antidepressant Overuse Debate," *BMJ* 2013;346:f191 (January 22, 2013), doi: http://dx.doi.org/10.1136/bmj.f191. Also see these other representative website articles: "Are Antidepressants Effective?" (http://www.webmd.com/depression/features/are-antidepressants-effective); Wikipedia's "Antidepressant," (en.wikipedia.org/wiki/Antidepressant); http://bjp.rcpsych.org/content/180/3/193.full;   http://healthland.time.

above, other models of disease have been postulated to explain symptoms.

---

com/2012/01/18/new-research-on-the-antidepressant-versus-placebo-debate/. Also see various debates regarding the release of the DSM-V. The push to focus on pathophysiology (biology and anatomy) as a means of explaining the behavior and symptoms of so-called "mental disorders" is fueled by several goals and the use of various technologies. One group of authors expressed the fact this way: "Establishing biological markers for diagnosis and treatment of depression is one of the most important problems to be solved in psychiatry practice" (*Nippon Rinsho 2003; 61 (9): 1667–1682*). To that end, the authors reported a reduced cerebral blood volume using a near infrared spectroscopy, one of the recently developed methodologies that can measure cerebral volumes simultaneously at multiple points with high resolution. The authors concluded that depression is characterized by a decrease in cerebral blood volume during a word fluency task. Similar claims have been made for other neuroimaging techniques in depression ("Positron emission tomography in depression: a neural systems perspective," Neuroimaging Clin N Am. 2003; 13:805–15). It is this type of information that only fuels the speculative fires regarding the potential cause of depression and attempts to move the physician away from filtering science and medicine through the grid of biblical truth.

In an editorial entitled "Is brain imaging clinically useful in psychiatry?", two sides squared off, represented by Dr. David Omen and Dr. Lois Flaherty (Internal Medicine News, June 1, 2006, p. 11). Dr. Owen said yes, based on some ifs: if mental disorders and aberrant behavior are related to functional brain problems; if single photon emission computed tomography (SPECT) imaging is a reliable measure of regional blood flow and activity. The question is: are they? Dr. Flaherty said no, that brain imaging remains a research tool. She said the data didn't justify its use and was concerned that brain imaging was being used to promise more than it could deliver.

The psychologization and medicalization of the community

As noted previously, it is quite striking how our culture is psychologized. Feelings, I remind you, are linked to thinking, wanting, and doing. In other words, thinking, wanting, and doing are *both* inner- and outer-man activities. Yet these simple biblical truths are so often ignored when ministering to people who are diagnosed with bad-feeling states, including depression. It is so easy to make a quantum leap and consider depression as a physical problem, that is, something wrong *with* the body. Rather, I am proposing that the problem of depression is most likely a problem *in* and *not* with the body. As I have said, proper definitions and terminology are critical for proper solutions. God's antidote for any feeling state and psychologized thinking is biblically-controlled thinking and wanting. From the patient-counselee standpoint, consider the following points:

- When most people speak of depression, they describe how they feel, using terms such as feeling down, blue, low, hopeless, depressed, discouraged, and overwhelmed. Feeling-directed behavior follows.

- Often they are not happy campers. Frequently they complain of fatigue and pain. They assume the problem is physical even though most, if not all, laboratory testing is normal. They assume that something is wrong with the body. On faith (not science), both physician and patient assume there is a brain problem, which it is assumed can be "corrected" by medications.

Therefore, people must be taught the following:

- Man was created a physical, sensual being. He receives input via his physical senses and interprets the input both in his inner man and outer man. As a result, feelings are generated that are real. We expect people to report these feelings; that is not the issue. Rather, the *source* of the feelings and the person's *response* to them must be addressed via biblical truth. The dual emphasis on the source and the response to feelings is essential in helping people get victory, both in the problem and in avoiding it.

- Man is *not* his feelings, but he does function as if he were. Feeling states say something about the person. His thinking and wanting are expressed in the context of God's providence and control.

- Bad-feeling states should not be a given for a believer. Often, however, a believer's thinking and wanting mirror that of the unbeliever. Frequently, the cry is that the situation *made* the person feel the way he does. The person, physician, and counselor attribute bad feelings to a physical condition that *needs* correction in some way other than *primarily* the application of biblical truth to the whole person.

- One person told me she was upset, but "okay." She was crying, and said she was nervous, depressed, and anxious. She reported these feelings (she did not mention thinking and desires) after a change in her circumstances: her husband had died and she was now alone. She was upset that her husband had left her and she was facing so many decisions and responsibilities. She was an overwhelmed and angry lady who sought relief by changing her circumstances and feelings. She said she loved the Lord and was confident in his care, but she needed medications because she had "a physical condition." The only evidence for her statement was her bad feelings.

- Christian physicians and biblical counselors must remind themselves, and teach others, the biblical truth that thoughts and desires—both inner and outer-man activities—drive feelings and actions. The whole person is involved in this response.

From the physician's standpoint, consider these points.

- Following the Medical Model of disease that they have been taught, many physicians automatically assume that a person diagnosed with depression has a physical problem. Yet the validity of the Medical Model for depression is still unproven. Therefore, these physicians are basing their diagnosis and treatment on hopes and assumptions, not on science.

- Many persons who display non-specific symptoms

without an objective cause undoubtedly will be labeled as depressed and given medication.

- Medications seem to be an appropriate choice, because patient complaints of bad feelings are so prominent and medications so plentiful.

When I work with people who have been diagnosed with depression, I assume nothing. I set aside the label of depression and the use of medications, and instead focus on the person by asking appropriate questions (see footnote 10). I ask them to tell me about the depression that they speak of rather than the depression they feel. Invariably, they tell me about their feelings; they do not volunteer their thinking and wanting. I inquire about their current thoughts and desires and those prior to the onset of their bad feelings.

Often I discover a pattern of thinking, wanting, doing, and resultant feelings of which they may or may not be aware. If they are aware, they often explain their reaction as "that's just the way I am." I ask them to tell me their thoughts and conclusions that they have drawn about themselves, their situation, other people, as well as the medications they may be taking. If the person is a believer, I ask them their thoughts about God, the cross, and their salvation and how those truths apply to them now. I want to know the person: their thoughts and desires. In that way, I will be able to minister the truth of God that is most appropriate for them, to the degree they will let me. Helping them put on the character of

Christ is pivotal in helping them get victory. I can only do that if I begin and end with biblical truth.

Let's return to the Bible to answer the query: Do *innocent* people experience bad feelings and inner-man angst? *Innocent* can mean "above suspicion," "blameless," "spotless," or "guiltless." Certainly Jesus was unblemished and spotless, but He was considered guilty by the Romans and the Jews, and ultimately by God (2 Cor. 5:21). We are told of His inner-man angst in several places (for instance, see John 11:33, 38; 12:27; 13:21). Some may say that Jesus was depressed. He had body problems. Did He have "spiritual depression"? According to Martin Lloyd-Jones, unbelief is at the heart of the bad-feeling state he calls "spiritual depression" (see footnotes 23 and 27). Certainly Jesus was not guilty of unbelief. If we agree (and I don't) that Jesus was depressed, we are forced to say that His depression was "physical"— something was wrong *with* Jesus's body that *made* Him feel the way He did. Those tempted to say that Jesus (and Paul) was depressed, usually define depression as "non-sinful bad feelings."

Often, they base their claim on the Medical Model, and postulate that something was wrong *with* (not in) Jesus's body. Today, this "something wrong" would be attributed to abnormal blood flow in the brain and the presence of various mediators, inflammatory cytokines, and neurotransmitters. These "abnormalities" would be considered *responsible* for Jesus's bad feelings. They made him feel de*pressed*. He would be considered a victim of

His body and His circumstances. Therefore, according to the Medical Model, Jesus would have needed medication (maybe even psychotherapy!) to correct the abnormality. Was Jesus depressed? No. Please read on.

Certainly, pressure and affliction were part of the fabric of Jesus's life and His whole person—He was a man of sorrows (Isa. 53:3–6). Did something on the outside of Jesus cause changes in His brain and its function? Where does biblically-controlled thinking and wanting enter into the picture? We are back to definitions. Can Jesus's body, *make* Him think and desire like an unbeliever at any point in His life? (see footnotes 16 and 24). I think not. To reiterate, we would do well to avoid labels such as "spiritual" and "physical" and the myriad of labels included in the DSM for depression. Rather, let's minister to the whole person using biblical truth.

Pressure and affliction characterized the life and whole person of Paul and Job (as well as others listed in the book of Hebrews, chapter 11). If unbelief is the key to spiritual depression, then those who are depressed are, at that moment, functioning as unbelievers and are sinning. The Bible agrees with this concept (see Eph. 4:17–24 and James 3:13–4:5; in each case, the author is speaking to believers). The same reasoning applies to worry (see Matt. 6:24–33). Worry is concern gone wrong. At its core, worry is unbelief.

Throughout the Bible, and especially in the Psalms, we are faced with people in various situations, often not of their own making. In that sense, they are innocent. Consider the book of Job. Job was judged by God as holy and blameless (Job 1:1.8; 2:3). He was marked by Satan as a prime target to *disprove* that God was the God He claimed to be. In this limited sense, Job was innocent. Satan attempted to discredit God through Job (1:8–12; 2:3–6). In each case, God initiated the conversation with Satan. God was in charge. In the end, Satan was God's agent (Job 2:3). God would be proved as true and good *or* false and bad depending on how Job functioned.

Did Jesus, the psalmist, and Job have bad feelings and inner-man turmoil? Yes. Were they depressed? I contend it depends on one's definition. My answer for Jesus is no. For others, I think we need to consider the possibility. A believer may depress himself, but he also can reverse the downward spiral of helplessness and hopelessness (see pages 75–77 and footnote 24, 26-27). He does the latter by clinging to and acting upon God's character and promises. The person does not pull himself up by his own bootstraps and in his own strength. Rather, because a believer has a proper reference to God, he counsels himself to think vertically, rest on, and apply God's truth in his present situation. He gets busy and productive. In the psalmist's and Job's case, sometimes a proper vertical reference was slow in coming. But it came.[34]

---

34   A word about Psalm 88: like Psalm 42–49, 84–85, and 87, Psalm 88 belongs to the collection of psalms ascribed to the sons of Korah. It is a lament, as many psalms are. It is the one psalm in which a

In summary, we please God as a whole person and we dishonor God as a whole person. Psychiatric labels, especially depression and the terms physical and spiritual depression, blur the Bible's emphasis on man as a whole person, a duplex being, and an image bearer of God.

What is Missing?

What is missing from the secular approach and definition of depression? The answer is multifaceted: it includes having and applying a proper biblical anthropology.

- Man is the image-bearer of God and is a whole person. Remember that the believer, as a whole person, is re-created in knowledge, holiness, and righteousness.
- God is a thinking Being. So, too, is man a *rational* being. The believer was created and re-created to *think* God's thoughts.

---

proper vertical reference seems absent. It begins with God but ends with darkness as the psalmist's closest friend. Apparently taunted by the refrain—"where is your God"—the psalmist believed the lie and failed to cling to God's promises. He agreed with those around him. In that sense, he became like them. See Psalm 73 for a similar picture but with a radically different ending because the psalmist came to his senses. Job had a similar "dark night of the soul" but repented when God confronted him. Coming face to face with the living God changes one's perspective and one's response to God and situations. Also see footnote 17.

- God is the Self-revealer. Man was created a *revelational* being, designed to correctly receive, interpret, and implement God's truth. Only the believer can properly function in this capacity.

- God is Lord and King and He is to be *worshipped*. Man was created a *religious* and *worshipping* being. The believer was regenerated and re-created to consecrate himself to God, not only in thought and action, but also in affections and desires. Only the believer *desires* to please his God, the eternal Triune God.

- God is an ethical, morally *responsible* Being. Man is morally responsible to God. The believer will function according to biblical truth as his standard for thoughts, desires, and actions, although imperfectly on this earth.

- God *relates* to Himself in the Trinity and His creatures. So, too, man is relational: vertically to God and horizontally to others.

- Man is a sensual being. He has feelings. He is not his feelings or his emotions. Feelings are directly related to thoughts and desires.

- Thinking, wanting, doing, and feeling are integral parts of every person, both in their inner and outer man. Each is linked to one another.

In contrast to a secular worldview and its standards, the Bible is primary, sufficient, authoritative, clear, and necessary when ministering to people in any state, especially feeling states. The Bible describes real people in real historical contexts with real problems who think, desire, and act as moral responders. The Bible describes people in particular situations via the providence of God, *and* it records God's answer for addressing the whole person including feelings (see Ps. 6, 13, 32, 38, 42–43, 32, 73, 77; the book of Job; 1 Sam. 1; 1 Sam. 30, Lev. 10:1–3; 2 Cor. 1:8–10; 4:8–10, 16, 18; 12:7–10).

A non-negotiable biblical truth is that God is for the oppressed, downtrodden, and needy (Ps. 9:9–10; 10:12–14; 18:27; 34:18; 68:5–6; 69:33; 72:2–6, 18–21; 146:5–9; 147:6; 149:4). These passages help us realize how easy it is to be led by feelings and experience. They point the person to the living God and urge a return to *and* a continued proper vertical reference, irrespective of feelings and experience. This one fact—that God is for the oppressed—was intended to motivate the psalmist and others to turn away from self, feelings, and experience and toward God, the great Deliverer. Jesus, the true Psalmist, did not lose this truth and His perspective. Therefore the believer is able to function as a Christian "oyster" and use what is unpleasant (pain) for gain (growth in Christlikeness; 2 Cor.5:9; footnote 22).

The Psalms are full of examples of individuals who demonstrated changed thinking and wanting. In each instance, the psalmist put off a wrong vertical reference and put on a proper one. Based on the truth about God and himself, the psalmist got busy praising God for who He is and what He has done and will do. The psalmist pointed to Christ, the true Psalmist, and redeemed the time and the moment (Eph. 5:15–18).

Because God is for the believer and the believer is united to Christ, Paul was convinced that no believer, in any circumstance, would ever be separated from God. God abandoned Christ at the cross, therefore it is impossible for Him to abandon the believer.

> Who shall separate us from the love of Christ? Shall trouble or hardship or persecution or famine or nakedness or danger or sword? As it is written: For your sake we face death all day long; we are considered as sheep to be slaughtered. No, in all these things we are more than conquerors through him who loved us. For I am convinced that neither death nor life, neither angels nor demons, neither the present nor the future, nor any powers, neither height nor depth nor anything else in all creation will be able to separate us from the love of God that is in Christ Jesus our Lord.
>
> – Rom. 8:35–39

In this passage, Paul addresses the foundational issues of all bad-feeling states: control and resources. In verses 33–34, Paul asked who would bring charges against and condemn God's people. His answer in those verses was not the Father or the Son. Who then? In verse 35, he lists seven "whats" that cannot separate believers from God. Yet he asks "who" will separate believers from God. The only "who" left is the believer (see verses 33–34). How can "whats" separate you from God? Paul's answer is that they can't. They are not the problem: the believer is the problem. Paul's point is that believers can and do functionally separate themselves from God in the midst of the "whats"—they depress themselves. Rather, believers are equipped to change and are to think and desire according to biblical truth. The change begins with one present thought and desire, especially as each relates to feelings in the context of the believer's situation.

God's answer for those diagnosed with depression is Himself. The person is to change their thoughts and desires. Even believers may deny that they can change. They have convinced themselves that the hole is too deep, and the mountain too high, and the feelings too bad. The change involves a patterned way of reacting and is often perceived as a daunting task. Thoughts and desires precede feelings, although most people deny the connection, because they are so accustomed to feeling-motivation and its results: feeling-directed behavior. For feeling-oriented people, changing thoughts and desires at the moment of pressure and as a patterned lifestyle is a major paradigm shift. Since believers are indwelt by the Holy Spirit, they can think God's thoughts and desire God's desires no matter how they feel. When they do, there is victory.

The Necessity and the Authority of the Bible

When faced with people complaining of bad feelings or diagnosed with bad-feeling states, the Bible must be used first and foremost. The Bible is not a medical textbook or a textbook for the diagnosis and treatment of physical problems. However, it does address and answer, either explicitly or implicitly, everything that a believer needs for life and godliness (2 Tim. 3:16–17; 2 Pet. 1:3–4). Scripture is all that a believer needs in order to properly *respond* to physical and non-physical problems. By definition, the believer is indwelt by the Holy Spirit, Who uses the Word of God to guide and to direct the believer to grow in Christlikeness. The Bible speaks authoritatively about stewardship, which involves taking care of the whole person. The Bible is the manual provided by God and preserved for the believer. It directs his path (Ps. 119:105). And since it does, Christians must r*everse* the paradigm of beginning with the culture's definition, explanation, and solution of feeling states and then moving to the person and the Bible. Rather, believers must begin with the Bible and move to the person. When faced with someone who complains of bad feelings and has feeling-directed behavior, believers must minister to the whole person.

Since the Bible is God's powerful, purposeful self-revelation, the pastor, biblical counselor, Christian physician, and friend must begin with <u>and</u> apply biblical truth to the whole person. As noted previously, one aspect of biblical truth is that every person is a rational, religious, moral being. He thinks, wants, and acts. *Circumstances* are the context of the moral drama played out in his heart (Prov. 4:23). Every person is in relation to God, properly or improperly, and they function, at any given moment, out of that relationship. Because God is Creator and man is creature, all of life is theological and every one of us is a theologian. The issue is, what kind of theologian?

A fundamental issue underlying depression (not simply bad feelings) are people's view of perceived lack of control and insufficient resources. They have believed and acted upon their feelings, experience, and own reasoning rather than the Word of God. They are convinced that their feelings won't let them act differently. Why shouldn't they think (feel) this way? People have been persuaded that bad feelings "just are" and that their presence precludes the regular and diligent application of biblical truth in the person's situation.

Progressive Sanctification is a Whole-Person Activity

What do salvation and sanctification have to do with thoughts, desires, actions, and feelings? Does the Bible speak about these topics? The answers are EVERYTHING and YES. Biblical truth always and completely trumps man's wisdom, especially that obtained by the triad of feelings, experience, and autonomous human reasoning. Christians, therefore, in order to appropriately minister to hurting people, must properly use the Bible in order to correctly reinterpret what the culture defines, describes, and treats. The culture focuses on feelings and feeling-directed behavior, and it equates emotions with feelings. The culture speaks of emotional breakdowns, but not broken feelings. Ironically, the secular scientific community does not agree on what an emotion is. Moreover, it does not tell us which emotions are "broken" or how they are broken in so-called "emotional breakdowns."

Feelings and actions always follow these thoughts and desires. Often the person may label himself—or be labeled—as having an *emotional breakdown.* In a so-called *emotional breakdown*, nothing is broken. In fact, the whole person is full of activity. While some may think it is descriptive to say a person is *emotional*, the term indicates that the person is functioning based on feelings. The use of the term *emotional* doesn't do justice to the Bible's view of the whole-person and the God who is in control of his world. Rather, the term depicts the person as reacting according to his feelings—driven by thoughts and desires.

Moreover, when one takes the culture's approach to so-called psychological problems, there is no real solution. Hope is only a *hope-so*, not a confident expectation of victory. It is to come through a variety of drugs

and psychotherapy. A person may feel better and therefore act better when taking medications. In the secular
system the terms "problem," "better," and "helped" are
defined and equated subjectively. "Problem" is equated
with bad feelings. "Better" and "helped" are equated
with a better quality of life and better feelings. The
person may feel less depressed. Their "black hole" may
seem less dark and their mountain less steep. The reality
of their situation may not have changed, but he or she
has better feelings. The same phenomenon may occur
when the situation changes by God's providence. Either
way, the pressure is off. Therefore, the person feels better.
In both cases, the person may act better because he feels
better. But there has been no real change in the person's
view of God, himself, or his circumstances.

Both patients and counselees have told me that being
on drugs *lets* them act (and think) in the way they did
prior to taking the drug. However, they are not as both-
ered by the situation or their reaction to it. Subsequent
situations that trigger bad feelings and feeling-directed
actions don't seem to stimulate the same thoughts and
desires. The person's response to the situation may have
changed. However, the person has not changed. He or
she is only affected by the medication, or more likely,
by a change in their circumstances. If the latter is true,
the context for exposing the person's inner-man is no
longer present. But if he or she has not learned to use
that which is outside of them to function as a Christian

"oyster," they will react in an unbiblical manner (see footnotes 7-8, 22, 25).

The believer was never in a "black hole" or facing an insurmountable mountain. Jesus has already entered and exited the hole and climbed the mountain in the believer's place. But the person who is labeled as depressed isn't influenced by those facts; consequently their thinking, wanting, and response doesn't change.

When the secular definition for the diagnosis of depression is followed, the DSM is the person's guide (footnote 14). Feelings are the major diagnostic criteria for the diagnosis of depression. They function as the person's authority for thoughts, desires, and action. They are the target for diagnosis and therapy, and their presence or absence determines the success or failure of treatment.

The question for the Church, for the Christian medical community, and for biblical counseling is this: How has the secular and psychologized approach to patients and counselees with bad feelings helped them grow in Christlikeness? My contention is that it has not and will not. However, once the person has received a label for his bad-feeling state, all is not lost. The pastor, biblical counselor, and physician can help the person dissect the label using biblical truth as their scalpel and following the principles I have discussed throughout this book.

The Requirement of a Proper Definition

Precise and correct definitions are critical in almost every endeavor. The medical community's definition for *depression* is based on subjectivity. It uses individual criteria for the diagnosis and assumes that if the person meets enough criteria, the diagnosis of depression is a given. The diagnosis for depression is based on several factors: the patient's self-reporting of "bad feelings"; feeling-directed behavior that is observed and/or recorded by medical personnel; and the medical personnel's interpretation of these two factors. These diagnostic criteria are allegedly based on science. So, again, I ask: Should we as pastors, biblical counselors, and Christian physicians accept the culture's view of bad-feeling states? Should we develop a counseling theology and methodology based on that view? Or do we derive a theology of bad-feeling states, including depression, from Scripture? The truth of the matter is that Scripture gives *no* formal definition of depression (nor does it give a formal definition of panic attacks, anxiety disorder, and anger disorder). As I have attempted to clarify, the Bible does address people with bad-feeling states. The Bible is the believer's tool—his scalpel—that addresses the heart of the matter: the person's view of God, himself, and his motivation for responding to situations, people, and ultimately to God. As Hebrews 4:12 says, "For the Word of God is living and active. Sharper than any double-edged sword, it penetrates even to dividing soul and spirit, joints and marrow; it judges the thoughts and attitudes of the heart." The above statements do not deny the reality of bad feelings and feeling-directed behavior. They do, however, motivate believers to view and use God's Word first, foremost, and completely as we minister to the whole person.

A third way is needed to minister to those with bad-feeling states. Depression is a whole-person phenomenon consisting of inner-man activity (thinking, wanting, and action and resultant feelings) and outer-man manifestations (bad feelings and resultant willful acts). Any definition that fails to consider man as a whole person, a duplex being, and an image bearer of God does not address man's thinking, wanting, and doing. Such a definition is not biblically valid. The converse is also true. Any definition that fails to address a person's thinking and wanting is not biblically valid.

The medical community would like us to believe that the whole (the diagnosis) is greater than the sum of the parts (each individual criterion). The converse is also true. Any definition that fails to address man's thinking, wanting and acting is not biblically valid. In other words, if a person meets enough individual criteria, then the diagnosis is made. For depression, the criteria in the DSM are descriptive and deal with feelings and observed, but also self-reported, behavior. Other conditions described in the DSM, such as Attention Deficit Hyperactivity Disorder (ADHD), also have criteria based on observed behavior. While the Bible does not give a definition of depression (or ADHD), the Bible certainly addresses each individual criterion that is used for the diagnosis of the various psychological disorders given in the DSM. Therefore, the whole is not greater than the sum of the parts. In his article entitled "A Biblical Critique of the DSM-IV," Dr. John Babler writes: "The core thesis of the DSM-IV is that there is a whole greater than the sum of the parts, a diagnosis, that explains the symptoms . . . This is an article on apologetics, on thinking biblically about how our culture thinks . . . My main purpose is to show that Scripture applies to the high-scientific sounding disorders by which people are labeled. The behavioral, emotional, and mental [i.e., thoughts, desires, and action–JH] criteria that make up each diagnosis are directly addressed by the Word of God."[35] I wholeheartedly agree.

---

35   John Babler, "A Biblical Critique of the DSM-IV," *The Journal of Biblical Counseling* 18, no. 1 (Fall 1999). Also see Rita Jamison's book *Parenting Your ADHD Child: Biblical Guidelines for Your Child's Diagnosis* (Greensboro, NC:

Moreover, the Bible describes people as they experience life: God's ordering of their circumstances. The Bible covers the whole range of the human experience. Therefore, it is more than reasonable—it is demanded—that pastors, biblical counselors, and Christian physicians begin with the biblical truth that everyone is a whole person (they think, they desire, they act), a duplex being, and an image bearer of God. A diagnosis and solution for any person labeled as depressed must begin with gathering data regarding the person's thinking, wanting, and doing and their relation to feelings.

Viewed from a correct understanding of the Bible's teaching about man, pastors, biblical counselors, and Christian physicians should confirm that depression, like other mental health disorders, is first of all an inner-man activity. That being the case, depression (as well as worry, fear, and sinful anger) is a bad-feeling state, a whole-person activity, that results from the person's focus on God and his providence in an unbiblical manner. This unbiblical focus is learned and practiced so that it becomes a way of life. Rightly understood, the DSM also defines depression as a whole-person activity, although its focus is on feelings. Since the DSM is a permanent fixture in our culture, I am in agreement with Dr. Babler

New Growth Press, 2011) and her pamphlet *ADHD: Helping Those Confronted with This Label Understand It and Evaluate Where They Need to Turn for Help* (Lafayette, IN: Faith Resources, 2006). Among other truths, these provide a biblical approach in addressing each individual criterion.

that the DSM needs to be reinterpreted according to biblical truth. Moreover, I contend that the *person* with a psychiatric label needs to be *reinterpreted* according to biblical truth.

As I have noted, depression is more than just bad feelings and feeling-directed behavior. Most people labeled as depressed by the DSM consider themselves resourceless. They consider themselves helpless and hopeless, with no way out of their situation. They are drowning in their feelings, which are often spurred on by a patterned lifestyle of reliance on a mindset of "I want" and "I deserve." The person believes, or "feels," that their resources are unsatisfactory and/or insufficient. They give up on God, biblical truth and its application, and their responsibilities as they give in to feelings.

The depressed person's desires and wants are not met, especially when he or she is faced with unpleasant situations. In response,

- <u>he</u> gives in to his feelings as <u>his</u> authority and guide;
- in varying degrees, <u>she</u> disregards and neglects biblical thoughts, desires, and actions;
- <u>he</u> functions less than God would have <u>him</u>, in whatever situation God has placed <u>him</u>;
- <u>she</u> does not apply biblical principles in a way that <u>she</u> should, given her circumstances and <u>her</u> position and relationship in Christ.

In other words, the core of depression is two-fold. First is the person's view of himself and his lack of control and resources, and second is the person's view of God: His perceived absence and/or His refusal or inability to act according to the person's wants, even demands.[36] The person feels that he is "under" the circumstances. His focus is on the circumstances as bigger than himself. As a result he thinks, feels, and acts overwhelmed. His desires and expectations (really his wants) are unfilled. He considers himself forsaken—alone and adrift. Bad feelings and feeling-directed behavior follow his wrong thinking and wanting. This person, who had considered himself to be in control, finds that "things" (God's

---

36   I have explained throughout the book that everyone is a theologian and that everyone has both a vertical (to God) and horizontal (to others) reference. Matt. 22:37–40 captures God's basic design for the believer. Moreover, man's knowledge has both a vertical focus (man's knowledge of God) and self-focus (man's knowledge of himself). The vertical and horizontal are linked, as are man's knowledge of God and himself. These truths are not new or original with me. Jesus emphasized this truth in Matt. 22:37–40. G. I. Williamson emphasized the whole-person activity of thoughts, desires, and actions in conversion: see footnote 4. John Calvin opened his *Institutes of the Christian Religion* (Book One, chapters 1–5) with the great truth that knowledge of God leads to knowledge of man and vice versa. John Murray, in *Redemption Accomplished and Applied* (chapter 4, pages 106–116), emphasizes that repentance brings about changed thinking respecting God, self, sin, and righteousness. So, too, true knowledge of God and self, rightly applied, are mandatory ingredients for getting victory in those having various psychiatric labels.

providential ordering of his life) are out of his control. He does not like it, and so he reacts sinfully.

When things are not to their liking, people can and do depress themselves. I remind you that the person labeled with depression brings a patterned response of thinking, wanting, and acting to every situation. A "me-first," self-pleasing habituation is a universal legacy from prior membership in Satan's family and kingdom. Dr. Jay Adams has referred to this phenomenon as *preconditioning:* a patterned lifestyle of thinking, wanting, and reacting based on feelings, which are the person's major instrument for interpreting circumstances.[37] Please

---

37   In his article "Counseling and the Problem of the Past" (*Journal of Biblical Counseling* 12:2, Winter 1994: 5–23), Dr. John Bettler wrote: "Present problems have a history, what Jay Adams initially mentioned as the 'preconditioning' level of a person's problems. The most comprehensive biblical phrase for how the past manifests in the present is used by Paul: the 'former manner of life' (Eph. 4:22). The 'old man' that the gospel [and grace–JH] progressively destroys is characterized by a lifestyle, a way of living, a walk, or 'walking' a manner of life. This manner of life is corrupt in what it believes, what it thinks, what it does, what it wants, as Eph. 4:17–19 and 4:22 drive home. Today's problems that bring people into counseling rarely emerge for the first time today. Patterns of life have been forged, practiced, and developed over the years."

In the accompanying footnote (page 118), Bettler wrote: "Adams discussed how the sinful disposition of the heart (desire-orientation, false beliefs, ungodly attitudes and values) manifests in *presentation* problems (often unpleasant emotions), *performance* problems (sinful behavior), and *preconditioning* problems (patterns of response that often go back to childhood): see *Competent to Counsel*, pp 148–155, 200–203."

remember that the terms *life, circumstances,* and *situations* actually are evidences of God's control in His world.

People labeled as being depressed are in a theological battle that centers on the application of *essential* and *simple* truths: God IS, they are, and they are dependent on His good and purposeful control. However, when depression is considered a physical problem, the significance of the battle is missed and denied. This line of thinking does not deny the fact that man is a sensual, physical being: he does feel. Two points are worth reiterating:

- The Bible brings clarity to man's true nature.
- Feelings are connected to thinking and wanting.

Functionally, those diagnosed with depression reject the above truths. Too often, those who care for them do likewise. The depressed person has dubbed his situation an "I don't like" situation. Bad feelings result. In fact, more often than not, a reactive, feeling-dependent response is patterned and habitual (though perhaps manifested in varying degrees). A response to God's providence is a response to God. For those diagnosed with depression, that response is based on a wrong view of God, His goodness and purpose, themselves, and the situation. As a consequence, the person so diagnosed considers himself or herself a victim to, and in, the circumstances. He or she assumes the self-defeating attitudes of "hang on," "cope," "accept," and "do the best I can." This only leads to misery and more bad feelings. As Proverbs 13:15 tells us: "Good understanding wins favor; but the way of the unfaithful is hard." (For a discussion of biblical endurance, see my book *Endurance: What It is and What It Looks Like in the Believer's Life*).

Yet so many patients and counselees, when presented with their reaction and the explanation described above, take offense (as do many physicians and counselors). They often deny their improper vertical reference, at least at that moment, claiming that they are victims of bad feelings, people, and "life." In reality, their claim is against God and His good, purposeful control. Some counselors who emphasize the person's suffering may think that my reasoning and interpretation of the Bible as given above and throughout the book is uncaring. However, believers and unbelievers are trained, and train themselves, to live by their feelings. Consequently they say "feel" when they really mean "think" or "want." In contrast, the Bible calls for biblically-controlled thinking (1 Cor. 2:16; 2 Cor. 10:5; Eph. 4:22–24; Phil. 4:8). Jesus preeminently taught and modeled the truth that thoughts and desires are linked, and that actions follow (John 4:31–34). Therefore:

- The person diagnosed with depression should be encouraged to do a spiritual inventory to determine the *source* of their bad feelings, which likely includes a patterned lifestyle of feeling-directed thinking, wanting, and doing.
- The spiritual inventory should include determining how

the person has *responded* to bad feelings. This two-fold approach is important to help the person get victory in the problem, to respond to the problem as a Christian "oyster," and to prevent future bad-feeling states.

• The person should repent as appropriate in their situation and for their maturity level as a believer. Specifically, at least, they should repent of using their feelings as their authority and guide, and for their feeling-directed behavior. Repentance is a friend to sinners, especially those who are led by their feelings.

• Someone may say that he is using biblical truth as his guide, but he still feels bad. With that statement, we are moving into the area of motivation. People often have mixed motivations. They may be motivated to please God but primarily to get what they want: which is usually good feelings. The highest and proper motivation to please God is God's worthiness—God deserves to be pleased. I ask people what their motive is for pleasing God: to get or to give? Pleasing God to get good feelings is, in essence, using God. Moreover, it won't lead to the *rest* that Jesus promises in Matt. 11:28–30.

• The person should be reminded that the proper use of appropriate biblical truth in order to please God does not guarantee good feelings or the absence of bad ones. But it does have its own reward, both now *and* eternally.

It simplifies life and carries with it contentment and peace (Matt. 11:28–30; Phil. 2:14–15; 4:10–13).

- The believer should be tenderly, yet firmly, encouraged to examine their view of God, themselves, and their resources. Having done that, they are to get busy pleasing God by using their bad feelings as their tool and God's instrument to please God. They are to function as a Christian "oyster" (see 2 Cor. 5:9 and footnote 22).

- A word about medications. As I have defined depression, medications are not indicated, yet so many counselees and patients will already be on medications when initially seen. It is not my responsibility or goal to change or stop medications. I will ask believers to tell me the reasons that led to the use of medications. I learn by gathering data. Unless their thoughts, desires, and actions have changed God's way for His glory, coming off medications will only lead to a return or an increase of bad feelings. As a result, the person, physician, and counselor will wrongly assume that biblical truth and its application have failed.

Conclusion

At least two non-negotiable truths stand out when addressing people who have been assigned psychiatric labels. Man is an inside-out person because of his duplex nature. He is a whole person who thinks, desires, and acts in his inner and outer man. People who display bad feelings and feeling-directed behavior and a diagnosis of depression must be evaluated based on a proper understanding of biblical anthropology. When that happens, the whole person will be considered—he or she won't be divided. Feelings, and people's response to them, will not be the major diagnostic criteria for depression or the target for medical treatment. Rather, thoughts and desires will be the target for the Christian *helper*—friend, pastor, counselor, and physician. Thinking and wanting will be evaluated using the grid of biblical truth in contrast to reliance upon feelings, experience, and unaided human reasoning as his source for reacting. Biblically-controlled thinking and wanting will replace sinful thoughts and desires. Biblical truth, rightly understood and applied, sets people free as they apply it to themselves in their situation. Of course, a person might demur, saying: "I can't, because I feel so bad." Pastors, Christian physicians, biblical counselors, and friends have heard that refrain so often. The same mindset is expressed in any situation in which problems are perceived as bigger than the person and God. Some of those problems may be a hard-to-live-with spouse, boss, or neighbor. Functionally, God is not in the person's thinking and if God is, He is only perceived as a pain reliever, a cosmic analgesic. Turning the person to the root and the heart of issue—their thinking and wanting in regard to their relationship with Christ—is the first step in helping the person get victory in their problems, not necessarily out of them. Victory, God's way, won't come until we view all feeling states from a biblical perspective.

For more information about
Dr. Jim Halla
&

Depression
please visit:

www.JimHalla.com
JimHalla@gmail.com
facebook.com/JimHalla

For more information about
AMBASSADOR INTERNATIONAL
please visit:

www.ambassador-international.com
@AmbassadorIntl
www.facebook.com/AmbassadorIntl